Praise for Rabbi Groner and Renewing Jewish Faith

"One of the greatest challenges for contemporary religious leaders is delivering a really good sermon—a message that is at once insightful and meaningful, concise and focused, respectful of the sacred text and the occasion, inspiring and relevant to the gifts and needs of the congregation. Having myself struggled to put words together for countless sermons over the past half century, I recognize a great sermon when I hear it.

Rabbi Irwin Groner has the special God-given talent of being such a spokesman for God's Word, a gift he has generously shared on a regular basis with his congregants at Shaarey Zedek for over four decades. Every word is carefully chosen, the imagery captivating, and the message heartfelt. As a frequent dialogue partner with Rabbi Groner, I know that his sermons from the High Holy Days will offer people of all religious backgrounds insight, challenge, and consolation. Rabbi Groner clearly knows and loves the Word of God; anyone who reads these sermons will readily share his passion and grow in love for the Almighty and his Living Word."

—ADAM CARDINAL MAIDA, Archbishop of Detroit

"Rabbi Irwin Groner is a man of great integrity who has helped shape the character of Jewish life. As a lifelong member of the Congregation Shaarey Zedek, I have always been inspired by the wit, wisdom, and sheer brilliance of Rabbi Groner's powerful sermons. Having them available now in book form will enable us to draw upon his insights as a continuing guide to the good life."

—WILLIAM DAVIDSON, Industrialist and Community Leader

"We come to the synagogue on the High Holy Days to ask for a favorable judgment from the Almighty on our lives for the years to come. For more than forty years, Rabbi Irwin Groner has guided the members of this congregation in these efforts and, particularly, enhanced their lives by his messages. I have been one of the beneficiaries of his words. I am grateful that they are now available for all to read in the years to come."

—HON. AVERN L. COHN, U.S. District Judge

"In sermons filled with beautiful stories and deep wisdom, Rabbi Groner draws upon his years of experience as one of America's leading rabbis to offer us a smile, some consolation, and messages that linger for a lifetime."
     —RABBI DAVID WOLPE, Author of *The Healer of Shattered Hearts*

"Rabbi Groner demonstrates in these addresses abundant wit, charm, humor, and insight. These sermons confirm his stature as a spiritual beacon who invariably captivates and inspires."
     —ROBERT SHAYE, Chairman and CEO, New Line Cinema

"Rabbi Irwin Groner has been preaching and teaching his people for over forty years, with fortitude and diligence. Rabbi Groner has much to show for his efforts, as evident in these sermons, each one carefully crafted, thoughtful and wise."
     —RABBI JACK RIEMER, coeditor of *Ethical Wills: A Modern Jewish Treasury*

"Some individuals, by their presence and leadership, lift the generations they represent, so that all whose lives come in contact with theirs walk on higher ground. Rabbi Irwin Groner is just such an individual. After reading this book, I am reminded of a passage in Scripture in which the voice of the Lord declares: 'Whom shall I send? And who will go for us?' Isaiah said simply, 'Here I am. Send me.' Rabbi Groner has answered a spiritual calling of his own, which he shares with his people."
     —HON. DAMON J. KEITH, Sixth Circuit Court of Appeals Judge

"In this treasure of wisdom and insight from Rabbi Irwin Groner, a distinguished leader of our Jewish community, we experience the equivalent of a sanctuary from which we can draw strength and acceptance of our individual circumstances."
     —HILDA GAGE, Michigan Court of Appeals Judge

Renewing Jewish Faith

Renewing Jewish Faith

Rabbi Irwin Groner

CONGREGATION SHAAREY ZEDEK

Copyright © by Rabbi Irwin Groner 2004
Published in the United States of America by
The University of Michigan Press
Manufactured in the United States of America
⊗ Printed on acid-free paper

2007   2006   2005   2004   4   3   2   1

A CIP catalog record for this book is available from the British Library.

Library of Congress Cataloging-in-Publication Data

Groner, Irwin.
    Renewing Jewish faith / Irwin Groner.
       p. cm.
    ISBN 0-974-92060-6 (cloth : alk. paper)
    1. Jewish sermons, American.   I. Title.
    BM740.3.G76 2004
    296.4'7—dc22   2004007889

*Every effort has been made to trace the ownership of all copyrighted material in this
book and to obtain permission for its use.*

Contents

🌿 *FREEDOM*

🌿 *FORGIVENESS*

🌿 *FUTURE*

Preface

Since 1959, it has been my privilege to serve as rabbi of Congregation Shaarey Zedek in Southfield, Michigan. During these three and a half decades, I have preached scores of sermons, but I have always steadfastly refrained from publishing a book of them, being conscious that the rhetoric of rabbinic discourse differs fundamentally from the style appropriate to the printed page. However, congregants and friends have suggested that these sermons, at least the most memorable, ought to be made available to a wider public and in a more permanent form.

The High Holidays offer the rabbi a superb opportunity to present the fundamental insights and values of Judaism in a popular form. One hopes that through the medium of these discourses, the laity may be led to a greater appreciation of and a deeper commitment to the Jewish heritage. I have sought to interpret the Jewish terms relevant to the modern age in a spirit of sympathy, for our generation is confronted with massive difficulties and great perplexities, virtually unparalleled in history.

This book addresses basic areas of concern in meeting the challenge of modernity. The book begins with a section designated "Folk" and addresses the issues of Faith, Family, Freedom, Forgiveness, and Future in subsequent sections.

The focus of these sermons, often stated explicitly, is the centrality of the synagogue in the renewal of Jewish life. The synagogue is that institution in which Jewish values achieve permanence. Here have been preserved the Jew's quest for justice, his passion for learning, his yearning for the messianic dream, his awareness of the Divine Presence, his celebration of life's sanctity, his reverence for hallowed seasons and sacred moments.

These affirmations are conveyed in the form of a sermon, which is not simply a speech delivered from a pulpit but is rather a distinctive kind of discourse, a spiritual ideal validated by sacred texts that proclaim its transcendental truth. A sermon addresses the core values of the audience, values that may have been forgotten or ignored. The speaker seeks to stir the conscience, to exhort and inspire his listeners. A sermon must also appeal to the intellect and should inform the "understanding heart." Thus, does a successful sermon kindle the flame of the spirit as it transmits its moral imperative.

The preacher of today knows that he was not appointed a divinely gifted spokesman of God's will, but he believes in the innermost recesses of his soul that he has entered the domain of the sacred. He is summoned to demonstrate his courage and wisdom in response to the challenge of modernity.

The sermons deal with Judaism as a way of life. The author argues that human nature cannot be understood exclusively in secular terms. The religious dimension of human existence must be understood as the basis by which life itself acquires meaning.

Every generation has been required to come to terms with religious belief. Our generation confronts the dilemma of American life, which is how to reconcile individualism and commitment. The American-Jewish community struggles to resolve this issue. That which is most precious to us is the spiritual heritage that has been enriched by the dedication and sacrifice of countless generations. That heritage might soon be lost by the attrition caused by forces of assimilation, acculturation, and intermarriage. And yet, Jewish life is flowering in this country as never before. The sermons give voice to both optimistic and pessimistic opinions about the future of Jewish life in the free world.

Judaism is the world's oldest religion, and its origin is in the dream of an ancient shepherd who taught that one God created the world and established the moral principles upon which the world could be perfected.

Two and a half centuries ago, the French philosopher Voltaire was engaged in a philosophic discussion with Frederick the Great regarding the possibility of miracles. The king of Prussia challenged the French thinker to cite one authentic miracle. Voltaire's famous answer was, "Sire, the Jews." We could respond similarly, for our age offers the best evidence of Voltaire's response. During the last third of the most brutal century in human history, when humanity was beset by a sense of hopelessness and defeat, one great and awesome miracle occurred—the survival of the Jewish people. This is most dramatically manifest in the birth and progress of the State of Israel and almost equally in the growth and development of the American Jewish community. These themes find expression in these sermons.

It is my hope that this volume will bring to both Jews and non-Jews a greater understanding of and a deeper appreciation for the relevance and insight of Judaism. May these sermons advance the ageless task that has been enjoined upon us by our tradition—to love all God's children and to be closer to the Torah. Yes, our very existence is a miracle, but that miracle was earned by centuries of loyalty and devotion, sometimes in the midst of unspeakable cruelty and hatred expressed by those who despise the moral teachings of the Torah. The Jewish people bear witness to their heroic character. In the teachings of Judaism, one discerns a clear and courageous faith in life, in God's love, and in man's potential. These sermons have one message expressed in different ways. Compassion, care, and love are not peripheral to a meaningful life. They are forces that make life worth living. With them, we have the strength and courage to meet life's crises; without them, we exist as less than human beings. Scripture declares: "The righteous shall live by his faith." Let such faith guide us and teach us how to live.

Dedication

This book is dedicated to my wife, Leypsa, who, for the past fifty years, has been a constant source of encouragement and inspiration and deserves a greater tribute than these words can express.

"She opens her mouth with wisdom . . ."
                    Proverbs: 31

Acknowledgments

I am grateful to A. Alfred Taubman, cherished friend, for making possible the publication of this volume by his generosity and support.

My appreciation goes to my Administrative Assistant, Shirlee Marshall, for her devotion and unfailing commitment to this project. Judy Haynes was of great help in this endeavor. I offer my appreciation to Chris Hebert of the University of Michigan Press for his skillful editing. I recognize with gratitude the wise suggestions of Rabbi Jack Riemer and his counsel, and the guidance of Christopher Tennyson.

The blessed memory of Ambassador David B. Hermelin endures in my heart.

Finally, I offer my appreciation to the men and women and youth of Congregation Shaarey Zedek for their support. They have opened their hearts in response to my concerns, my hopes and my dreams. Their voice can be heard in every sermon.

About the Author

For four decades, Rabbi Irwin Groner has been the spiritual leader of Congregation Shaarey Zedek in Southfield, Michigan, one of the largest Conservative congregations in North America. As senior rabbi, he distinguished himself as an author, a communal leader, and a public speaker. In 2003, he received the Rabbi Simon Greenberg Award for Distinguished Rabbinic Service from the Jewish Theological Seminary. He won recognition for his role as president of the Rabbinical Assembly and for his work as chairman of the "Etz Hayim" Publication Committee that produced the acclaimed commentary on the Torah. His sermons, essays, and articles have been widely published.

Rabbi Groner chaired the Rabbinical Assembly conventions in 1976 and 1977 and cochaired the National Youth Commission of the United Synagogue from 1972 to 1976. In 1984, he was appointed by then governor of Michigan James Blanchard to serve on the Judicial Tenure Commission, the first clergyman appointed to that board. He has been actively involved in interfaith programs in metropolitan Detroit and served as president of the Michigan Board of Rabbis.

Rabbi Groner is the product of a distinguished rabbinic family in Chicago. He holds degrees from the University of Chicago and the Hebrew Theological College of Chicago. In 1982, he received an honorary doctorate from the Jewish Theological Seminary.

Rabbi Groner and his wife, Leypsa, reside in Southfield, Michigan, and are the parents of Hon. David and Hon. Amy, Dr. Joel, and the late Debbie Groner.

FOLK

No people in the world has presented such a vivid example of unwavering perseverance and unflinching devotion to faith as the Jewish people. No nation has exerted so mighty a religious influence on humanity as Israel. Their Bible is by far the greatest book among the holy books of nations, and it makes the Jews "God's People."

—JULES BARTHÉLEMY SAINT-HILAIRE,
French philosopher

There is a people that dwells apart, not reckoned among the nations.

—NUMBERS 23.9

Why Be Jewish?

We live in an age of incredible opportunity in which everything can be changed, from hair color to body type, from nationality to religion, from career to spouse. We spend more on diets than most nations spend on food. We must be all that we can be. The word *impossible* is not part of our vocabulary. We are offered an array of choices available to no other age in the history of the world. We shall spend our entire lives immersed in this world of few limits and seemingly infinite possibilities.

When "new" means "better," we feel we cannot rely on the traditions, values, and institutions that we inherited. In the wake of these changes, we often feel that the sense of purpose that was once our Jewish patrimony has evaporated. The heritage of the past is no longer binding upon us.

It is no wonder that amnesia is the new Jewish disease. We raise money for our causes but no longer know precisely why. In an era of marketing, we fumble for words when asked why we are Jews. We become mute when questioned about the content of this identity. To what are we committed other than the continuity of people who call themselves Jews?

One notes the irony in this latest crisis. It is the result of a long-standing Jewish dream finally coming true. For centuries, Jews longed to live in a society in which we would be seen as ordinary human beings. We wanted to succeed. We dreamed of tolerance, understanding, and equality.

Why Be Jewish?

The dream has finally come true. In America, Jews have found a society that accepts us, for almost all vocations and neighborhoods are open to us. In this age, in which Jews can freely choose Judaism, they can also choose to be part of something else, or nothing. Jews need not convert out of Judaism—they can simply drop out. We have new questions. What does it mean to be a Jew? What do the Jewish people stand for? Do we have an obligation to remain with the Jewish people? Where does that obligation come from? What does Judaism offer that I cannot find in a secular society? We have reached the ultimate question. Why be Jewish?

No longer can we take it for granted that our children will love and cherish the heritage of their ancestors. No longer can we presume that the reasons for being Jewish are both compelling and self-evident. Now, as never before, we must be able to formulate for ourselves, and for those we care about, reasonable, meaningful, honest responses to the question, Why be Jewish?

This is a most radical question. Our ancestors, who had to cope with oppression and persecution, did not ask, Why be Jewish? Victims of the world's hatred, the outcasts among the nations, they did not ask, Why be Jewish? But the modern Jew, who lives in the comfort and ease of an open and integrated society, who enjoys the greatest privileges of any Diaspora community, asks, Why be Jewish? And then he issues a challenge. "Prove to me that there is value and benefit to being Jewish. Otherwise, I may opt out."

No longer are we Jewish because the majority religion denigrates and vilifies us. No longer are we Jewish because we suffer and because we are reviled. No longer are we Jewish because we have no choice.

In recent years, I had a conversation with a college student who was bright, articulate, rebellious, and alienated. I quote his comments from memory: "Rabbi, being Jewish was always important to my parents. But I cannot see any rational basis for perpetuating that parochialism for myself. Why should we ghettoize an entire group of people away from the mainstream of our society? I feel that we should all consider ourselves human beings and not subdivide ourselves into clans and religions. In truth, this is not merely my personal view. Many in my generation cannot see why it is important to remain Jews."

I have pondered his statement. This sermon is directed to that student.

Where once Jewish identity and commitment were nearly impossible to escape, we must now argue for every soul, we must convince every mind, we must persuade every heart.

Finding Answers

If we fail to find answers, then the Jewish present and future will seem meaningless to the next generation. Jewish history, and its story of sacrifice and martyrdom, will appear as a tragic waste, one huge cosmic mistake.

One student forces us to confront this question. If our children or grandchildren had a choice, would they choose to be Jewish? Are we giving them the kind of home, the kind of Jewish values that make them want to continue living as Jews? Do they understand, and do we, what it really means to be a Jew, beyond a Brith Milah, beyond Bar or Bat Mitzvah, beyond two seats for the High Holidays, preferably in the sanctuary? If physical threats to Jewish survival have diminished, why does Judaism need us? And, if Judaism does not truly shape our values, why do we need it?

Surveys and Statistics

We seek comfort in surveys and statistics. They don't provide us with much *nachas*.

Picture a patient on a hospital bed, just before surgery. He asks, "What are my chances, Doc?" The doctor smiles, "100 percent—not a worry in the world." "How do you know?" asks the patient. "Easy," replies the doctor. "Nine out of ten die as a result of this operation. My last nine patients died, so that means you are going to be just fine."

Sometimes it is very hard to comprehend the statistics about the future of Jewish life. Is the fact that the rate of outmarriage is higher than it has ever been the bad news; or is the circumstance that it is reassuringly lower than that of any other ethnic group in America the good news? How are we doing as a Jewish community in terms of loyalty and retention?

One may argue that the question, Why be Jewish? is only theoretical. History has often shown that we have no choice, for the Gentile world sees to that. Whether the Jew likes it or not, the outside world has not been slow in reminding him who he is and whence he came.

The story is told of Otto Kahn, the New York banker, who was walking in the street with Marshall P. Wilder, a humorist who was also a hunchback. On Fifth Avenue, Kahn points to a magnificent building. "Marshall," he says, "you see that church? That's the church I belong to. Did you know I once was a Jew?" "Yes, Otto," replies his companion, "and I was once a hunchback."

But the world has changed. Professor Mordecai Kaplan once pointed out that "the Western world gives the Jew the freedom not to be Christian without the power to be a Jew." Today, in America, there is no external force of anti-Semitism that is powerful enough to compel Jews to remain loyal. But, in any event, I don't want to remain Jewish just because the non-Jews won't let me be something else. I want to feel that I should be able to say, as did Walter Kaufman, the Princeton philosopher, "If I were about to be born and could choose what people to be born into, I would say that I should like to be a Jew."

Why be Jewish? I offer several responses, recognizing that this existential question is not easily answered.

The Holocaust

First, we are to be Jewish because of the Shoah. Some months ago, I heard a man who had survived the Auschwitz and Bergen-Belsen concentration camps say, "After what the Nazis did to us, we must never give up our Judaism. We must never forget the six million." We are aware that the Jewish tradition contains 613 commandments. Emil Fackenheim, a contemporary Jewish philosopher, declared that the 614th commandment is that the authentic Jew of today is forbidden to hand Hitler yet another posthumous victory by letting the Jewish people die.

It is not accidental that foreign dignitaries making their first visit to Israel are obliged to visit Yad Va-Shem. The profound impact of the Shoah on Jewish young people has been demonstrated by countless educators. The film *Schindler's List* should be seen by all our youth. Holocaust memorials are significant parts of the landscape of Jewish contemporary life. We must live to remind the world of its potentiality for inhumanity; we must endure in order to say Kaddish for the six million. So many Jews died because they were Jewish that we, who live much more privileged lives, do not have the right to abandon their memory. "Zachor," or "Remember," is the moral imperative of our time.

I affirm these principles with all my heart, but they are not sufficient reason for our young people to be Jewish. They have no historical memories of Eastern Europe, nor do they feel this urgency. If our youth have no other sources of Jewish inspiration, the Shoah is not sufficient cause for them to be Jewish. Our college student could say, "I'm tired of being persecuted and hated and despised. The pain of my ancestors is not enough reason to remain a Jew." The Shoah allows our youth to be angry about the tragedy of the past without having to face up to the challenges of Jewish life today. Modern Jews will make Judaism a part of their lives if it is relevant and meaningful for their present and future, not because of an unspeakable tragedy endured and concluded long before they were born. Either Judaism will speak to their souls and their hearts, or they will stop listening.

Let us consider other approaches.

Judaism and Ethnicity

Some people point to ethnic identity as the way of being a Jew, a cultural heritage that distinguishes us.

Young Jews have said to me, "Rabbi, I'm not a religious Jew. I'm an ethnic Jew. Jewish customs and folklore and foods are part of my life. That's why I'm still Jewish." To that comment, I reply that you no longer have to be Jewish to enjoy Jewish ethnicity. Dennis Prager pointed out that once, when he was eating in a restaurant in Los Angeles, he chuckled when he heard a black waitress explaining to a Japanese tourist from Tokyo what matzo balls were. William Safire points out that in American cuisine, the consumption of bagels has now passed that of doughnuts.

What is distinctively Jewish ethnic food anyway? "The Jewish people have observed their 5,736th year as a people," the Hebrew school teacher informed her class. "Consider that the Chinese have only observed their 4,692nd. What does that mean to you?" After a pause for reflection, one boy raised his hand. "It means that the Jews had to do without Chinese food for 1,044 years."

An Enduring People

Why be Jewish? The next response is the claim of peoplehood. We owe it to our fellow Jews to identify with the fate and destiny of Jews everywhere on the globe. We affirm our continuing membership in the Jews as a distinctive, evolving people.

Jewish life provides something that is profoundly lacking in contemporary life. We feel that sense of community when we assemble in the sanctuary and join the many others sharing in worship and observance.

An individual's joy is the joy of us all. Personal sorrow is the pain of the many. The concept of Minyan is, after all, the experience of community in action. We laugh, we cry, we pray, we study, we celebrate, we believe, we doubt, we dream, we build—personally to be sure. But, in the final analysis, the Jewish self acquires its fullest meaning in community.

I saw bumper stickers a few years ago that were part of the Christian revival movement. The stickers bore three words: "I found it." One Jewish wit proposed that our appropriate response—if indeed any response was needed—would be, "We never lost it." The faith of Israel is not the faith of individuals but the faith of one people through history.

Why be Jewish? We are today's links in the long chain of the Jewish past. Judaism is where we came from. Being Jewish is the debt we owe to our ancestors.

We say to the next generation, "You owe it to the Jewish people not to leave us. We are so few that every one of us is precious. We can't afford to lose anyone." But we neglect to offer them anything in return. We forget to tell them of the wondrous benefits available to them in this entity we call Jewish tradition. Instead, we build on their sense of guilt. We seek to shame them into Jewish loyalty, a strategy doomed to failure.

Israel and Jewish Identification

Why be Jewish? Our next response is founded on the single most powerful source of Jewish identification of our times, the State of Israel. For many Jews in this last half century, Israel has been the primary answer to the question, Why be Jewish? The drama and energy of the Zionist dream have inspired and engaged Jews of diverse backgrounds in many different ways. Israel remains an essential source of Jewish self-confidence and identification. Arthur Hertzberg, an astute observer of Jewish life, has put it this way: "Israel is indeed the center of Jewish loyalty . . . not only as a cause to be supported, but as a place whose existence helps to make Jews more comfortable and secure in America."

Israel has done so much to inspire contemporary Jewish existence; to mobilize Jewish energies; to reclaim the Jewish homeland; to enable Jews to assert their historical role as a sovereign, independent people. The existence of Israel as a Jewish state provides the ultimate response to the Holocaust in which the Jew could be but victim. Pride in the accomplishments of Israel today is a central pillar of Jewish identification. It is important to send our young people to Israel in their teen years and beyond, to be inspired by the glory of Zion rebuilt.

But Israel in and of itself cannot sustain life in the Diaspora for the generations to come. Israel is not our *nachas* machine and cannot be expected to be the sole source of Jewish meaning for North American Jewry. In the everyday conduct of their lives, American Jews maintain little substantive connection with Israel. Israel cannot fill up our void. We cannot live a vicarious Jewish existence and find the strength for Jewish renewal in North America. There must be more!

The Jewish Contribution to Civilization

Why be Jewish? The next response summons us to Judaism because we have made an astounding contribution to civilization. Quantitatively, the Jews are slightly less than .35 percent of the world's population. More Chinese are born each year than there are Jews living in the world today. But it is quantitatively that Jews have made, and continue to make, an incredible contribution to mankind in literature, poetry, philosophy, the physical sciences, music, art, psychiatry, law, government, commerce and industry, and academia. Why? How do we interpret this phenomenal Jewish intellectuality, accomplishment, and generosity? Why so many Jewish scientists, physicians, technological virtuosos? This tiny percentage of the population of the world has earned almost 27 percent of the Nobel Prizes. How do we explain this? Did these people of prominence attend *heder* when they were young? Were their homes intensely Jewish? I doubt it. But something of Judaism rubbed off on them, if not from the influence of parents, then their grandparents.

But how convincing is this argument for our skeptical student who asks, "Why me? Why am I expected to enrich world culture? Moreover, so many of these intellectual giants were only marginally Jewish. Besides, my achievements will belong to me, not to the Jewish people."

Are there no other answers to why be Jewish? I offer another answer of a different kind. We should not evade it. It presents God as the source of meaning of Jewish existence.

The Torah's Answer

Why be Jewish? The answer is found in the Torah reading of Rosh Hashanah, which declares that God charges Abraham with a mission: "All the nations of the world will be blessed by your descendants." Our answer, therefore, is that we have a purpose, a task, a mission to perform. We have transmitted to the world those values from which Western civilization stems. We have been the teachers of mankind. We have given the world the concepts of God and ethical monotheism. We have offered the Torah; the Talmud; our sacred literature; our heroes, sages, saints, and martyrs. Wherever the Jew wandered, a people without a country, during two thousand years of the Diaspora, they brought a spiritual message to every land in which they settled: the Jewish commitment to learning, justice, and compassion; to the sanctity of the family and the ennoblement of character. Many taught *kedushat chayim*, the sanctification of life. That explains why we must be Jews, because we have something unique to give to the world for the benefit of mankind.

The Jew who lacks conscious knowledge of his past and the will for Jewish survival becomes a meaningless deviant from the majority. But the Jew who knows why he is and why he wishes to remain a Jew stands out as the embodiment of a thousand years. He partakes in a sense of divine mission to mankind, which has ever been the glory of his people.

The wondrous story of the Jewish people has not reached a conclusion. Judaism is not a song that is solemn; it is a continuing symphony which each Jew may either swell with harmony or mar with discord. It is the symphony which echoes forth to the world.

Our mission was described in the Torah read last Shabbat. The text declares: "Not with you alone do I make this covenant with its sanctions, but even with those who are not here with us today—even with all the future generations."

Sinai is the answer to the question, Why be Jewish? We all entered the Covenant. We were all at Sinai, even those of us who don't remember and even those who joined the family later. Sinai incorporates all the other partial answers. We, the Jewish people, may not be able to recount the details, but we do believe that we heard God speak and that we received the Torah. After we reached Sinai, we were never the same again. We built a society and a people the likes of which others never even considered.

Why be Jewish? Stand at Sinai and feel the awesome revelation of the Divine Presence, and you will understand. The truth is that, beyond the answers, beyond the theological interpretations, Jewish life transcends rational explanation. It is built on faith. It is a matter as much of the heart and soul as of the intellect.

Ultimately, the question, Why be Jewish? cannot be satisfactorily answered with words alone. It has to be experienced. It becomes real to Jews when they live it, not when they simply think about it. That is why we must provide rewarding, stimulating, challenging Jewish experiences in afternoon religious schools, the Jewish Academy, Hillel day school, family education, United Synagogue Youth, Camp Ramah, trips to Israel, Chavurah, campus Hillel foundations; in the resurgence of participation in adult Jewish study; and much more. Judaism can excite the mind and answer the deepest hungers of the soul.

Why be Jewish? I believe that commitment to Jewish life will revive our spirits, rekindle our passion for living, and infuse our lives with joy and meaning.

This is our message to the generation of the future. Do not abandon the religion that is yours by birth, the faith of your parents and ancestors. Judaism is your inheritance. Its people are your people.

> We need you to be Jewish.
> The world needs you to be Jewish.
> God needs you to be Jewish.
> You need to be Jewish.

A Personal Decision

The rationale for Jewish survival is ultimately an intensely personal one. A Jew knows instinctively the importance of Jewish continuity, although it might require a lifetime of exploration to explain it even to himself. The search may in fact lead you to take a class, join a cause, take a trip to Israel, read more, study more, daven more, learn Hebrew. The most persuasive reason for being Jewish is the satisfaction you can find in taking part in the all-encompassing life of the Jewish people.

It is time for us to affirm ourselves, our authentic identity, to affirm who we are and for what we stand. Being Jewish is not a problem to be solved, and Judaism is not a condition to be cured. It is a celebration of life, a most precious gift. Our heritage is rich with insights and observances, visions, texts, spirit—a veritable treasure providing meaning and direction for ourselves, our families, and our community.

If Jews do not care about Judaism, who will? If Jews cease to be Jews, who will represent this vision of a higher purpose of life to the world? I address my student. "Friend, the real answer to the question, 'Why be Jewish?' has to do with you. If you choose to disregard your Jewish heritage, you will lose something of supreme value that cannot be replaced by anything else."

Why be Jewish? Because there is still a long road ahead of us to finish what we began to do. The spiritual struggle continues. We began to teach, but our teaching is not yet fulfilled. Therefore, once and for all, Jews should make up their minds that we are a living people and we want to continue to live.

I believe that the day will come when Jewish existence will be exalted in a redeemed and renewed world. Until that glorious day dawns, every succeeding generation of Jews must declare, "I will not die, but I will live to declare the glory of God." Our purpose is clear. Our destiny is revealed. May our wisdom and our faith match our great challenge.

Grant Honor Unto Thy People

On this Kol Nidre night we fix our gaze on the Jewish people, and we consider its destiny, its uniqueness, and its future.

There is a prayer recited in the Amidah of this High Holiday season at every service that is a source of puzzlement: "U'vchane tane kavod l'amecho"—"And therefore, oh Lord, grant honor unto Thy people."

What sort of prayer is this? We pray for life, we pray for sustenance, we pray for forgiveness, we pray for security, we pray for peace. But honor? Does not Judaism emphasize humility, self-abasement, the absence of pride? Dare we, on these solemn days of moral striving and introspection, address God and ask Him for honor, and beseech Him for glory? Is not vanity the source of much evil, conceit the root of transgression?

But the tradition placed this petition in the forefront of our liturgy with great insight and with just emphasis. For a sense of honor is essential to human life—indeed, without it life becomes unworthy and valueless. With it, we regard ourselves or we are regarded as worthy of esteem. In the classical tragic works, like *Oedipus Rex,* the hero who dishonors himself in his own eyes spiritually dies with the loss of his self-respect. What self-respect is to an individual honor is to a people. No people will endure, no people will create, and no people will triumph without a sense of honor.

For the Jew, honor was elusive. He had a glorious past, marked by the valorous achievements of kings, the moral passion of prophets, and the brilliant wisdom of sages and poets. But the long dark night of Galuth brought upon him the contempt of the nations, the derision of the peoples, and the ridicule of the world. There is a haunting phrase in the Siddur: "Habet mishomayim ur'ay"—"Look down from heaven and behold, for we have become the mockery and the scorn of the nations . . . and in spite of it all, Thy name we have not forgotten."

The Jew cried out not only for the physical persecution that he suffered at the hands of the Roman Empire, the church, the Moslems, the crusaders, the Cossacks, the Inquisition, the czars, and the Nazis. He wept because of the dishonor: the walls of the ghetto, the yellow badge, the peaked hat; the stereotypes of Judas and Shylock and Fagin; the discriminatory legislation; the "perfidious Jews" for whom prayers were offered; the constant humiliation.

Do you remember an old Yiddish song "Eli, Eli"? It resonates with the pathos and the passion of the centuries of Jewish suffering, endurance, and hope. "Eli, Eli—My God! My God! Why hast Thou forsaken us? With fire and flame they tortured us. Everywhere they made us to shame and mockery."

That is why the prayer book includes the supplication "U'vchane tane kavod l'amecho"—"And therefore, oh Lord, grant honor unto Thy people." At this season of judgment when the Jew prayed for himself and for all mankind, he voiced the fervent plea that his shame would cease and his degradation would end when the promise of redemption would be fulfilled for him and for all men.

But Jewish history bore a secret aspect, a hidden dimension that the world did not perceive. Despite his inferior station and his contemptible existence, the Jew had a sense of honor that was independent of and impervious to the opinion of others. He respected a standard of conduct which was uniquely his own. He had his own measure of what life should be, his own definition of virtue, his own conception of success, his own scale of values. These standards were fashioned by his history, his tradition, the activities of his daily life, and the moral code of his own community. His tradition taught him, from his earliest youth, that he was descended from a people chosen by God to play a unique and redeeming role in the history of mankind. When he read in the Talmud that the seed of Abraham is "compassionate, modest and committed to deeds of loving-kindness" he knew by what ideals he was to live.

The great Hebrew poet Hayyim Nachman Bialik tells in one of his poems how, as a small boy, he remembers his father teaching him Chumash and Rashi in a tavern, the same smoke-filled saloon his father kept to make a living, for this was one of the few occupations in which Jews were permitted to engage in czarist Russia. What a powerful and eloquent image is evoked by that poem. Surrounded by vulgarity, corruption, and ignorance, the Jewish father taught his son Scripture and the teachings of the sages. Such has been the glory of Jews. In the midst of corruption, we preserved an island of holiness.

A sense of honor is expressed in what one will not do. Even among thieves a shred of honor is sometimes left. They will not inform on one another. Generally, the more things we will not do, the keener our sense of honor. Through the ages, our forefathers would not compromise their faith, they would not deny their heritage, they would not surrender their morality and their self-discipline, they would not betray their love of God and man. In external matters, they stooped to endure all kinds of humiliation. In affairs of the soul, they maintained their self-respect.

The Jew measured the world against his own standards of honor. In medieval and even modern times, a sense of honor was the prerogative chiefly of the aristocracy. Only they had the right to defend their honor, for example, in a duel. Men of rank settled their personal quarrels with weapons. Hence the phrase "to give satisfaction," which means that either blood must be drawn or one of the contestants must die. For the Jew this was not honor, this was barbarism.

Heinrich Heine was an assimilated Jew who saw the contrast between his writing and that of Cervantes, who created the character of Don Quixote, the romantic figure of knighthood and chivalry. Heine said of Cervantes, "My colleague mistook windmills for giants. I see windmills in our industrial giants. He mistook a leather wineskin for a crafty wizard, and I see only a leather wineskin in our modern wizards. He mistook every beggar's inn for a castle, every donkey-driver for a knight, every stable-wench for a court lady. I, on the contrary, look upon our castles as paltry inns, our knights as donkey-drivers, our court ladies as stable wenches. Just as he mistook a puppet play for a state affair, so do I hold our state actions to be a pitiful puppet play."

The Jew stood apart from the world of knighthood; of feudalism; of military duels between nations; and of the nobility, real and spurious, that was born from that system. Jewish wit often pokes fun at those values which belong to such systems of honor. There is an anecdote of a Rothschild into whose Frankfort office the duke of Gramont enters. "Take a chair, Baron," says Rothschild. "I am the duke of Gramont," remarks the indignant visitor, having expected a more princely welcome. "Take two chairs," says the banker.

The Jewish aristocrat was not an expert swordsman; a knight of King Arthur's court; a straight shooter; or indeed, a man who excelled in violent contests. The Jewish gentleman was best described in the Fifteenth Psalm: "Lord, who shall sojourn in Thy tabernacle? Who shall dwell upon Thy holy mountain? He that walketh uprightly, and worketh righteousness, and speaketh truth in his heart; that hath no slander upon his tongue, nor doeth evil to his fellow, nor taketh up a reproach against his neighbor; in whose eyes a vile person is despised, but he honoreth them that fear the Lord."

On this Kol Nidre night the questions we must ask ourselves are, What honors us as Jews? What shames us as Jews? If we can answer these questions we shall understand what we are and what we must do.

What honors us as Jews? Israel brings us honor. That same Hebrew poet, Bialik, to whom I made earlier reference, wrote the poem "The City of Slaughter" after the Kishinev pogrom, which plumbs the depth of his grief and the intensity of his emotion. After the poet depicts the tragedy of the pogrom and the brutality of the mob, he portrays the self-humiliation of the victims at the feet of their persecutors and their

utter incapacity to contemplate any form of defense. With a defiant bitterness, Bialik exclaims, "I take a solemn oath, in the name of Almighty
God, that I shall not cry, and I shall not allow my eyes to flow with tears,
for great is the pain but even greater is the shame."

The State of Israel bestowed a great gift upon world Jewry. It
removed from us the shame of our collective helplessness. Are we honored simply because Jews now have an army, a navy, an air force? This
is not the source of our exultation. Israel reversed a two-thousand-year-
old role of the Jew on the stage of history. For the past two millennia
the Jew's external history had been shaped for him by other nations.
There is, therefore, a motif of helplessness and passivity in all of his
wanderings and experiences. The creation of the State of Israel means
that we have achieved self-determination as a people and, thereby, self-
respect. In their ancestral land, which Jews redeemed themselves, they
now determine their own destiny, and they are building a society which
is founded on the principles of justice, democracy, and ethical sensitivity—ideals which were proclaimed by the prophets of that country and
the sages of that people centuries ago.

We take pride in the achievements of the Six-Day War. The Israeli
people did not exult in the military victory in the style of a conquering
nation. When the war was over, there were no celebrations in
Jerusalem, no parades in Tel Aviv. There were no brass bands and military exercises to commemorate the occasion. There was relief, and
there was mourning for the dead. The most moving statement of that
time was made by Golda Meir, who said, "Someday we will forgive the
Arabs for killing our sons, but we will never forgive them for making
our sons kill them." No such statement was ever issued by the leader of
any country following a brilliant military victory. But we are Jews, and
we live by a different sense of honor. Honor is not encountered in
destroying life—honor is discovered in saving life.

There has recently been published a book called *The Seventh Day*, a
fascinating record of the feelings and experiences of the Israeli men
and women who fought the Six-Day War and whose frank answers were
taped and transcribed. A doctor describes the following episode: "We

were approaching an oasis. A large number of Egyptian soldiers came
out of a big house, formed ranks and put their hands up. Suddenly, I
noticed that one of them could scarcely stand. He was on the point of
collapse and had an infected wound in his right leg. I called him over
and told him to lie down. There was a sudden silence among the Egyp-
tians. They thought he was going to be killed. Then they saw me put
him down on the floor, open my pack and take out bandages, alcohol
and clean the wounds. Suddenly they saw something they didn't understand. An Israeli officer kneeling on the ground, attending to an Egyptian private who was filthy, full of pus; not simply an officer tending to
a private, but an enemy officer taking care of his enemy. This was something completely beyond their understanding, and just as previously
there had been dead silence among them, now they suddenly shouted:
'Ya'ish Israel!'—'Long live Israel!'"

"Who is powerful?" Ask the sages. "He who transforms an enemy
into a friend," they answer. This is our conception of valor. May such
victories be multiplied, and may such conquests be enlarged so that the
dream of peace for Jew and Arab can be realized in the Middle East.

We are honored by the valor of Jews in the Soviet Union. For over
fifty years a generation and more of Jews were raised under the discipline of a totalitarian regime which sternly forbade Jewish instruction
and made Jewish observance and contact with world Jewry all but
impossible. How could there have occurred such a surge of passionate
yearning to be Jewish, to live among Jews, to share in the building of
Israel? Where do our brethren find the unbelievable courage to declare
themselves publicly as Jews loyal to the Jewish people and to Israel? It
was recently announced that more trials of Jews will be held in
Leningrad, Kishinev, and Riga. A group of fifty Russian Jews have
recently sent a petition to the Presidium of the Soviet Union protesting
these trials and asking that the defendants have the free choice of attor-
neys and demanding that the foreign press be granted permission to
visit the trial. And these fifty submit their names, their cities, and their
addresses. A saga of heroism is being enacted before our eyes that
reflects honor on the Jewish people. There are names that have now

entered the annals of heroism of our history—Boris Kochubyevski, Grisha Feigin, Rivka Alexandrovitch, and Mickhall Zand. Each of these and hundreds more tell the story of an individual fighting for freedom, for dignity, and for self-respect with an undaunted spirit and a fearless heart against the power of a totalitarian state.

The reports from Russia describe a continuing resistance against Soviet cultural genocide. Hebrew is being studied in Moscow in an underground ulpan. Broadcasts of Kol Yisrael are taped and transmitted from one secret group to another. Petitions to go to Israel issued to foreign governments are openly signed and published.

There is a story of a Jew who was standing in line in Russia waiting for a pass to visit Israel. This Jew had once before been given a permit to visit. When the official saw his renewed application, he remarked, "So you don't like our Russian republic very much. You seem to find Israel more attractive."

"Oh, no," said the Jew, "I find things in Russia very fine. There is only one thing missing. In Israel, every morning at seven o'clock the milkman rings the bell."

"What is so wonderful about that?" asked the Soviet official. "In Russia, every morning at seven o'clock, the milkman rings the doorbell, too." "Yes," said the Jew, "but in Israel, I know it is the milkman."

During recent summers, groups of young people of Conservative synagogues around the country, the United Synagogue Youth, accompanied by rabbis have visited the Soviet Union and met with Jews wherever they can be found. The stories one hears are amazing.

An American girl walked down a Leningrad street. She noticed a number of students, and she wondered if there were Jews among them. She began to hum the anthem of the Jewish people. Suddenly, as though all had been prearranged, a group formed around her and defiantly began singing "Hatikva." The American leader cautioned the Russian youth that they might be noticed by the authorities in this public place. They answered courageously, "We don't care who sees, who knows, who informs. We are Jews. We shall be reunited with our people. Am Yisrael Chai."

In spite of the personal risk, Russian Jews coming to Israel appear with Jewish symbols, with a Magen David embroidered on their neckties or with the map of Israel etched on the faces of their watches, and they speak Hebrew.

Dr. Abraham Joshua Heschel once recounted an ancient Jewish myth about the ten lost tribes of Israel. They have not disappeared; they dwell beyond a legendary river, the Sambatyon. It is a river that is impassable and impenetrable. He pleaded, "Shall we permit a Sambatyon River to separate us forever from a major part of world Jewry? Shall the Russian Jews, whose courage and self-respect have redeemed Jewish honor, be reduced to the plight of the ten lost tribes?" Let us solemnly resolve that we shall not forget them. We shall proclaim before all men that we demand justice. We shall be their voice. We shall arouse the conscience of decent men and women everywhere. We shall encourage our brothers in their heroic struggle to challenge their oppressors. We shall awaken the world, for in the struggle of Soviet Jewry we and the people of Israel are honored.

I could end this message having expressed what I believe is an important element of Jewish self-understanding. But there is something missing. What about American Jewry, what about us?

The Jews of this country have worked their way from a generation of poverty-stricken immigrants to positions of influence, importance, and leadership in sixty years. We have played a significant role in the social progress of America. We can take pride in our community, in our institutions of learning, of religion, of benevolence, of healing, and of welfare. We have produced leaders—men of spirit, dedication, and insight whose names are part of the saga of contemporary Jewish history.

But Yom Kippur is not a time for self-congratulation and for complacency. This is a period for critical self-examination, painful though it may be, a time for confession and for disclosure. As a rabbi, I am deeply disturbed by what is happening to our personal lives; to our sense of honor as Jews; to that moral excellence which had, through the ages, been our guide and our ideal. There is, in our age, a decline in the adherence to those standards and values by which Jews have traditionally lived.

Consider the Jewish family. Even our most vicious, hate-filled enemies have admitted that the Jewish family was a fortress of purity and decency and fidelity through the ages. That fortress is being breached from within, as we see Jewish homes without Torah, without ideals, without reverence. Divorce, infidelity, and coarseness are sapping the strength of *sh'lom-bayit*, family harmony and sanctity. All over the country colleagues corroborate my own experience that the fabric of Jewish family life is weakening. A broken Jewish family a generation ago was a rarity. Today, it is becoming a commonplace.

A man of honor can be recognized when he says "no." He rejects that which corrupts, debases, and degrades. Mattathias and the Maccabees said "no" to the violence, the nakedness, and the depravity of Hellenistic culture. If we live with a Jewish sense of honor, we will say "no" to that which has become decadent in American culture—its obscenity, its violence, its lewdness, and its paganism.

But there are some among us who have said "yes." Everybody else is doing it—the non-Jew is no better. After all, they argue, didn't we struggle for the right to be the same, to be equal with others?

We, as Jews, have no monopoly on vice, no exclusive franchise on immorality. But we are different—at least we were. If we were like all other peoples, we would have vanished long ago. We live by a Covenant; we live with a message; we live for a purpose. The truth of our existence is sealed in our flesh. It is not that the Jew has to be better than others. Let him live up to his own standards—of honor, of virtue, of self-discipline.

I am greatly disturbed about what is happening to some of our younger people and to some who are not so young. Judaism is not prudish about sex. Judaism recognizes the sanctity, the force, the life-affirming power of the sexual impulse. No cult of celibacy was ever accepted by Judaism. But sex is being abused and dehumanized by some among us. It has become for them a form of amusement, a diversion from boredom, an occasion for conquest, a pagan orgy. Thus does life become cheapened, and marriages are broken, and the spirit is dishonored.

Several years ago, in developing a similar theme, Rabbi Morris Adler expressed his concern about the decline in Jewish sobriety. He referred to the fact that "we have begun to drink; we are now very well represented at bars."

The problem today, seven years later, is far more grave. Drug abuse and narcotics addiction have entered wide sectors of the Jewish community. If some monstrous fiend would have murdered twenty young Jewish men and women from the ages of eighteen to thirty at the rate of two a month over the past year, a wave of indignation would have swept the city and would have ended such a horror. Twenty died, and the fiend was, directly or indirectly, overtly or covertly, the abuse of drugs. There were a few cries of alarm; then apathy and indifference descended. I weep for these young people. I weep for their parents. I weep for us, for as a group we are all dishonored; none of us is without some share of responsibility in these deaths.

The drug problem is insidious. It begins with marijuana, which seems relatively innocuous but which may be and often is the first step in a self-degrading process which includes stimulants, depressants, hallucinogens, and narcotics. I fear that this contagion has become epidemic in its proportions in some areas of our collective life.

We must, as a community, mobilize our resources to meet this tragic problem. We must, as parents, guide, influence, and protect our young. Young people should be encouraged to live by a sense of honor so firm and so compelling that they can say "no" to every corruption, "no" to every foul temptation, "no" to every lure to self-destruction. A Jew who lives with a sense of honor knows that not everything that is possible is permissible. Unrestrained self-indulgence is possible. Infantile self-gratification is possible. The lustful pursuit of sensual pleasure is possible. Experimentation with mind-expanding drugs is possible. Selfishness, self-indulgence, and evasion of responsibility are possible. But not everything that is possible is permissible. A man of honor says "no."

If we forget this, we who carry the name Jew will be as a messenger who has forgotten his message, as a witness who has forgotten his testimony, as a man of rank who has forfeited his honor.

At the conclusion of his book on Jewish history, Abba Eban cites the following quotation: "A nation is a soul, a spiritual principle. To have a common glory in the past, a common will in the present; to have done great things together, to want to do them again—these are the conditions for the existence of a nation."

We have done great things together. I believe we want to do them again. Let us strengthen our will and fortify our spirit for the tasks of the present—for in our hearts is the vision of ancient splendor, a prophetic dream of man uplifted and society redeemed. In our hands is the torch of a brilliant flame fed by faith, bestowed upon us by generations of greatness. Let us hold it aloft proudly. It is our burden, but it is our glory. "U'vchane tane kavod l'amecho"—"And therefore, oh Lord, grant honor unto Thy people."

The Everlasting Covenant

When does a Jew feel most Jewish? On Kol Nidre night. Even the most estranged and distant among us, if he possesses the smallest spark of loyalty to his community and his God, wishes to be in the synagogue on this night. All of us are there: the devout and the doubtful, the saintly and the skeptical, the dedicated and the dubious. On what other occasion do such multitudes gather as Jews? When else do we lay aside our personal concerns and our daily pursuits and dedicate ourselves to our common goals and aspirations as a people? Our presence in the synagogue is itself a profound statement of Jewish affirmation and loyalty. It connects us with the ancient beginnings of our people, the events that define our destiny.

In recent weeks, we read the sidra of Nitzavim, which describes how Moses addressed the Hebrew people before his death. He set before them a message that he wished to impart with such emphasis that it would remain with them for the rest of their lives. "You are standing this day, all of you, before the Lord your God; your leaders, your tribes, your elders, your officers, even all the people of Israel, your little ones, your wives, the stranger, and even the lowliest, the hewer of Thy wood and the drawer of Thy water."

What is the purpose of bringing the entire people together? "It is that thou should enter into a Covenant of the Lord, Thy God, unto His oath, which the Lord Thy God maketh with you this day." We are struck by the chutzpah of Moses. He proposes that this motley group of erstwhile slaves enter into a Covenant with God and that this physically bruised and emotionally scarred horde is to be designated as "Am Kadosh," a holy people. The chutzpah is even greater. Moses declares (vs. 13–14), "It is not with you alone that I make this Covenant and this oath; because I make it with him that standeth here with us this day before the Lord, our God, and also with him that is not here with us this day."

What does this mean? Who was not there? Furthermore, how could those not present be included in this agreement?

It is important that we understand this text, for it is fundamental to the comprehension of the total experience of the Jewish people. The crucial term is *brith*, or Covenant, standing alongside such words as *Torah, mitzvah*, and *tzedakah*. *Brith* defines the mutual commitment between Israel and God. The brith makes Israel a priestly people, for God has called that people to His service.

Who is this Jewish people that ratified the Covenant? Without verses 13 and 14, we might say that those who entered the Covenant were those present when Moses called this solemn assembly—six hundred thousand and more. However, the Torah declares that the Covenant bound those who were there and also those who were not there. Who was not there? All the generations that were yet to come, all the unborn souls of the centuries of the future. Our ancestors were there, our grandparents were there, our parents were there. Even though we live three thousand years later, we, too, were present when the Covenant was ratified, for a direct line of commitment joins us to the promise of our ancestors. We march by the same orders; we fall under the same obligations; we are connected by the same historical event.

The Covenant defines our relationship to each other. In the days of European Jewry, two Jews, strangers, met on a train in Poland. One says to the other, "I know you from somewhere. Do you come from Minsk?" "No." "Did you ever do business in Lodz?" "No." "Have you ever traveled to Cracow?" "No." "Well, we must have met at Mount Sinai."

Consider this definition of a Jew: "A person who never meets a fellow Jew for the first time." We were together somewhere, or our cousins were, or our ancestors were.

Now this notion may seem to you an extravagance of imagery. But, in a profound sense, it is true. Our personalities, outlook, and values were determined by the tradition defined by that Covenant—the Torah. We are the original partners to that tradition. We are not only inheritors, but we are also founders. We are not only descendants, we are also ancestors. This sense of sharing the very beginning of the Covenant is simultaneously the mystery, wonder, and miracle of Jewish existence.

Never mind that you did not give your own word in person. To be a Jew is to be born under the weight and the glory of a sacred promise, a promise that endures through all the generations. Or does it? My description could fit the medieval Jewish community, or the organic Jewish community of prewar eastern Europe, or the shtetl. But does this image portray the typical congregation of today? Are we part of that ancient promise, or has modernity separated us from all that came before?

Woody Allen recounted that "in school when they asked for my religion, I knew I was in trouble. I answered, 'Jewish, with an explanation.'" For the modern Jew, none of the traditional answers are sufficient "without an explanation."

The transformation of American society has been good for American Jews, who have flourished as never before. But what about the wellbeing of Judaism? Will the openness of American society mean Judaism's gradual withering away?

In the past, Jews remained Jews for one of three basic reasons: because they believed that was what God demanded of them' because they were born into an organic community with powerful sanctions and rewards, or because anti-Semites would not permit them to become anything else.

None of these factors function in the same way today. We are aware of anti-Semitism, but thank God, there is no longer enough of it to hold the community together. Nor is being Jewish something that is forced upon Jews by their own community. With regard to belief in a God who makes demands on them, American Jews range from agnostic to Hasidic, from skeptic to Satmar.

In choosing to remain as Jews, American Jews have, in their way, renewed the ancient Covenant. We have reached that moment in history when we are the first generation able to choose whether or not we shall be Jewish of our own free will. American Jews have responded without hesitation or doubt, casting their lot with their brethren all over the world. We are one with Jews of the free world, with Jews of Israel, with Jews of Moscow and Leningrad and the "Refuseniks" languishing in Soviet prisons. Because of the Covenant, we are a fellowship reaching horizontally to every corner of the earth and reaching back in time to the promise of Sinai.

American Jews, in choosing to remain Jews, have reaffirmed and renewed the ancient Covenant. The impact of this decision was dramatically portrayed in this true story. Louis D. Brandeis, the first Jew on the Supreme Court, was a very bright law student at Harvard University. In those days, Harvard had a very exclusive honor society, to which no Jew had been admitted. Every day for lunch, Brandeis had uninvited company. Someone from the society would join him at the table and say, "Brandeis, you're brilliant, so brilliant that you may someday end up on the Supreme Court. But you are Jewish. What chance do you have? Why don't you convert to Christianity, and all your problems will be solved."

At the beginning of his senior year at Harvard Law, the leaders of the Honor Society invited Brandeis to membership.

The evening of his official induction arrived, and Brandeis was asked to speak for a few minutes. He walked to the lectern, slowly looked around the room with his piercing eyes, and said, "I am sorry I was born a Jew!" Applause, shouting, and joy greeted that statement. "Finally, we convinced him," the society members said to each other.

When the room was quiet, Brandeis spoke again: "I'm sorry I was born a Jew, but only because I wish I had the privilege of choosing Judaism on my own!"

Each of us chooses to be a Jew. American Jews enter the Covenant through different paths. We affirm the Covenant by adhering to the traditional framework of Jewish law and observance. We affirm our loyalty to the Jewish people and uphold our responsibility to the State of Israel and, in that way, take the Covenant upon ourselves. We determine to transmit Judaism to our children and our grandchildren and thereby renew the Covenant. Whatever path we choose, we discover that it is in the renewal of the promise made at the beginning of our history that we discover who we really are.

Where do we find the strength to affirm the promise? When a Jew enters the synagogue, he renews that Covenant which is at the very center of Jewish history. He expresses by his presence his freely willed choice to accept the ancient vow and the age-old pledge. The synagogue is the only institution which articulates the enduring meaning of Jewish existence. The synagogue preserves our memory of the past and our hope for the future. The future of world Jewry and Judaism itself is dependent upon our will to live as Jews, a determination inspired by the faith of the synagogue.

Israel is a fundamental commitment of the American Jewish community. World Jewry relies upon the support of American Jewry. That support will continue in years to come only if we rear a Jewish generation that will say as other Jewish generations in the free world have said, "Ani Yosef achichem—I am Joseph, your brother. We are one people; we share a common history; we are linked by a shared vision."

It is a common mistake to believe that the synagogue is a gathering place for saints. It is not. If it were, it would not be so crowded. The synagogue is our spiritual home. As we enter, we are reminded of who we are, and to whom we belong, and of where we once met.

What troubles us as parents about our children is a haunting question: Will they carry on? Will they be ours?

Some years ago, when Golda Meir was prime minister of Israel, a group of American Jewish leaders met with her in Jerusalem. At the conclusion of their discussion, their leader turned to her and asked, "What is your most important concern?" Leader of a country surrounded by enemies; beset by many difficulties of absorption, defense, and nation-building, Golda Meir paused for only a second and responded, "My most important concern is: will your grandchildren be Jewish?"

Our today will soon become yesterday. What tomorrow are we helping to create? Will our children and their children and the children beyond them inherit the precious legacy that we possess? Will they be able to say when they read the Book of Deuteronomy, "Yes, we were there too!" May we be able to answer that question for the future with honor and integrity.

The opportunity is ours; the time is urgent; the reward is great!

We Are All Israelis Now

On September 11, enemies of America inflicted on this nation the worst act of terrorism we have ever experienced. Before last week, it would have been hard for us to imagine anything more cruel than the bombing of the Federal Building in Oklahoma City with 168 dead. The casualty numbers out of New York City and Washington will probably be thirty or forty times as great, the equivalent of an Oklahoma City bombing every day for a month.

We have to talk about it because it is on everyone's mind and lies so heavily on everyone's soul. It has been hard to think or talk about anything else for the past week. We have to talk about it although it is hard to find anything to say except how much it hurts and how angry we are.

I remember, when I was a boy, we would begin the Rosh Hashanah service with a prayer whose opening words were "May the old year end with all of its calamities, and may the new year begin with all of its blessings."

I recall that that prayer always made me uncomfortable. I would say to myself, "That prayer belongs back in Europe where life was hard and every year brought more trouble. But here the years are good." But in these days, I find the ancient words poignant and evocative, and I find myself praying that all the killing, all the hatred, all the tears and bloodshed of these past days and months should vanish along with the old year and that, in the coming year, we are free of all that.

But what is there to say? How does one make sense of a senseless tragedy? How does one come to terms with the knowledge that some people hate other people so much that they would kill themselves in order to kill thousands of strangers?

After the terrible events of last Tuesday, a number of colleagues I spoke to had all independently come up with the same insight. They said, "We are all Israelis now because all Americans know the feeling of vulnerability, of uncertainty. They know how Israelis feel when they go shopping, when they send their children off to school in the morning, when their sons and husbands leave for military reserve duty. And if we are all Israelis now, maybe we can learn something from Israel's fifty-three years of hard-won experience dealing with the threat of terrorism."

How do Israelis handle the danger? They go on living. They continue to shop, they continue to ride the buses, they continue to send their children to school. They understand that if they ever stopped going on with their normal lives, they would be conceding the field to the evil ones, and they are not willing to do that.

How can you live in a world where you say good-bye to your loved ones in the morning and you can't be certain you will ever see each other again? People are saying to themselves, "Where can I move to? How can I change my way of life so that I don't have to be in danger?"

I believe the Israelis have given us the answer. They have rejected yielding to the threat of terror. They have squared their shoulders, summoned up their courage, and gone on with their lives.

I have heard a great deal of anger, which is understandable, and a desire to get even with whoever has done this to us, which is understandable.

Occasionally I have heard or read people suggesting that maybe we should moderate our support of Israel so that we shall no longer be a target for terrorist hatred. I want to say unequivocally that those people are wrong. Muslim fanatics don't hate us because we're pro-Israel, and they wouldn't stop hating us if we were less pro-Israel. They hate us because we stand for democracy; for gender equality, treating women as full human beings; for freedom of speech and worship; for values that they are terrified of. This issue cuts even deeper. To change our foreign policy because of terrorist acts is to reward and encourage more terrorism. It is another way of yielding power to the evil ones. It is like feeding your friends to the tiger in the hope that the tiger will eat you last. It is what weak and powerless countries do, not strong independent ones. And I pray that our government, like the government of Israel, never shrinks to that point where it would do that. Don't let the terrorists win.

A second concern is how we as a nation will respond to what was done to us. Ever since Tuesday, we have felt hurt and angry and helpless. There seemed to be so little we could do to help the victims or to hurt the perpetrators. And when a person feels helpless, there is an almost irresistible impulse to do something to reclaim power, to restore a feeling of being in charge. The danger to America is that, out of our pain and rage, we will forget what we stand for as a people. We will betray those values that our enemies hate us for.

On Wednesday and Thursday, stories began to be published about some of the people who died in the planes and in the office buildings. There were faces and stories to go with the names and the photos. Many people can't comprehend the Holocaust when they only hear the number six million. They have to read *The Diary of Anne Frank* to understand what was lost. That is the reason for confronting our mortality, because it is at this time that we face up to the unsettling truth that none of us knows how long we have to live. It is decreed on Rosh Hashanah and confirmed on Yom Kippur who shall live and who shall die—who by sword, who by fire. Did you ask yourself when you read those words? Do you believe that God decided last September that these thousands of people would not live to see another autumn, that the terrorists were doing God's will? This is obscene. I think the prayer comes to us to warn us that because life is precarious, make sure you start doing the things that really matter—the deeds that will ultimately win you your immortality.

Ever since Tuesday, America, like Israel, is at war. A war against an enemy whose face is difficult to see but whose fist is painful to feel.

The final numbers are not in yet. But the loss of life was incredible. The injuries will leave scars on the souls of thousands of people. And the loss of the sense of safety and security will be felt from now on by each of us.

There is one thing we know for sure, and we have the pictures to prove it. We all saw those pictures of thousands of Palestinians singing, dancing, celebrating on the West Bank. We will not forget those pictures for a long time to come, because they demonstrate that we are now in a holy war against those who hate us, against those who hate all modernity and all liberalism and all freedom and all of anything but their own narrow-minded fanaticism.

What shall we tell our children? We don't know what to tell ourselves. I only hope and pray that this attack will teach us what it should, which is to renew our determination to live by our values.

Let me ask a hypothetical question. If you had seen that plane that attacked the World Trade Center, and if you had had a rifle in your hand, and if you had shot it down before it struck the building, would you be considered an assassin or a hero? The answer is obvious. Anyone who could have shot that plane down should have. And anyone who did so would be considered a hero, not an assassin. We know that now, but we didn't know that a week ago. Up until last Tuesday morning, the American government routinely condemned the Israelis who struck back or who did what they had to do in order to prevent such attacks. Up until Tuesday morning, the State Department routinely condemned the people who retaliated by aiming their weapons not at women and children but at those who planned and led those attacks. Up until last Tuesday morning, the State Department called these people assassins. Not this week, because this week, we are all Jews, we are all Israelis, and now we understand the wisdom of Israel's policies.

I pray that in time we will heal, we will unite in sadness and mourning but not in fear. We will go forward from this moment. I sought to provide words that would help make some sense of that which troubles the American soul. And I thought of words that I would address to the enemy, to the unknown author of this suffering, to the demon who saw the fulfillment of this diabolical scheme. And these are the questions I would address to the enemy.

What lesson did you hope to teach us by your cowardly attack on our World Trade Center and our Pentagon? What was it you hoped we would learn? Whatever it was, please know that you failed.

Did you want us to respect your cause? You just damned your cause.

Did you want to make us fear? You just steeled our resolve.

Did you want to tear us apart? You brought us together.

Let me tell you about my people, the American people. We are a vast and quarrelsome family, a family rent by racial, social, political, and class division. But a family. And although we walk through life with a certain sense of blithe entitlement, we are fundamentally decent, peace loving, compassionate. We struggle to know the right thing and to do it. And we are, the overwhelming majority of us, people of faith and believers in a just and loving God. We are not weak. We are strong in ways that cannot be measured by arsenals. Are we in pain? Yes. We are in mourning; we are in shock. We are still grappling with the unreality of the awful theme, still working to make ourselves understand. Your attacks are likely to go down as the worst act of terrorism in the history of the United States, probably of the world. You have bloodied us as we have never been bloodied before. But there is a gulf of difference between making us bloody and making us fall. When roused, we are righteous in our outrage; we are terrible in our force. When provoked by this level of barbarism, we will bear any suffering, we will pay any cost, we will go to any length in the pursuit of justice, and I tell you this without fear of contradiction. I know my people, as you do not.

Our character is seldom understood by people who don't know us well. As Americans, we will weep; as Americans we will mourn; as Americans we will rise in defense of all that we cherish.

So, I ask you again: What was it you hoped to teach us? It occurs to me that maybe you just wanted us to know the depths of your hatred. If that's the case, consider the message received.

And take this message in exchange.

> You don't know my people.
> You don't know what we're capable of.
> You don't know what you just started.
> But you're about to learn.

I wish to speak briefly about Israel's situation. It is a difficult war for Israel to fight. There is one more reason why this is a difficult war to wage, because North American Jewry seems to behave as if it is not just six thousand miles away from Israel but sixty times six thousand miles.

I remember; Israelis remember; you may remember how in 1967 and 1973, we, the Jews of North America, identified heart and soul with Israel. We took to the streets by hundreds of thousands in order to demonstrate on Israel's behalf. We came out of the woodwork in order to identify with a cause. We gave money in breathtaking amounts. We went to Israel to express our solidarity. But this year, none of that happened. Very few North American Jews came to visit Israel. They didn't seem to care. And Israel has felt very much alone because with some exceptions, we Jews seem to be indifferent to their cause.

A colleague and friend, Rabbi Jack Riemer of Florida, wrote to Rabbi Shlomo Riskin in Efrat, and said to him, "Tell me what I should tell my people when we meet this year on the first day of Rosh Hashanah." Rabbi Riskin wrote back, and I quote: "We Israelis feel very lonely; we feel let down by the North American Jewish community because we are in the midst of a difficult war of survival and we don't hear you—and we don't hear from you." Rabbi Riskin said that he had to come to America this summer in order to raise money for Eilat—not for the schools of Eilat. "I came in order to raise money with which to buy bullet-proof buses so that our kids can go to school in safety. And I came in order to raise money to buy bullet-proof vests, children's size, so that our kids can wear them when they go to school each day."

What do we need to feel? What do we need to know? We need to feel proud of Israel. Are you aware that even during this year of bombings, and sneak attacks, and many acts of murder on the roads, do you know that forty-five thousand Jews came to Israel from the former Soviet Union and some Jews—I don't have the exact number— came to Israel from Ethiopia? Ethiopia? When the nations of Europe and Africa assembled in Durban, they said, "Israel is based on Zionism. Zionism is a form of racism, and, therefore, Israel should not even be allowed to go to the conference." Do you know that no African state, no black state, was willing to take a single person from Ethiopia, even though those people are suffering from drought? Israel took people from Ethiopia. Not one European state was willing to take in a single person. None of the countries that went to Durban and voted to call Israel racists were willing to take a single Ethiopian. Israel did, in the midst of a war. We should feel incredible pride in Israel.

So, finally, what should we do, we who live here, who exist in safety and in tranquility? One thing I know for sure. We should not despair. It is forbidden for a Jew to despair. Each morning during these Days of Awe we recite twice daily Psalm Twenty-seven, in which we read,

> The Lord is my light and my salvation, whom shall I fear?
> The Lord is my life's strength, whom shall I dread?

We know to the core how fragile life is, how unpredictable life is, how we are all linked by the bonds of human frailty and longing for a better and safer world. Now is the time when we need each other's strength. We need each other's courage. We need each other's love. We pray for the victims and their families, for the strength and resolve of the nation, and for the wisdom of our country's leaders.

Tuesday was a day of stunning calamity. Our tradition teaches us both how to deeply mourn and how not to despair. And yet, we are coping with deep emotions. We are angry at the terrorists who have been nurtured on such hatred that this bred this dastardly deed. We are angry at the countries who harbor them and have funded them for so long. And we are angry at ourselves for allowing this to happen. And only now, our president has awakened us to the need to punish these terrorist states themselves, and we know who they are. We are also angry at so many Western countries who, unlike the United States, did not support Israel at that conference in Durban and allowed the Arabs to take over and call Zionism racism.

Where can we look for comfort? We look to God, and we assemble in prayer, seeking His help. But we have seen that we can also look within. We have seen thousands of acts of true bravery and kindness over these past days, and they continue. But I don't think any of us will truly feel any real relief until justice is done, until those who trained these suicide pilots are punished, until the governments who funded them are punished.

There is profound evil in the world. There is the evil that seeks to destroy us all with no distinctions of religion, politics, age, gender, status. It means to rob us of our way of life, to obliterate our civilization, to annihilate our way of life because of a demented, deranged, and lunatic fanaticism that repudiates all that we hold sacred and dear.

This was an attack on Western civilization. This was an attack on human freedom, which this country best represents. This was an attack on a pluralistic society that accepts everyone. This was an attack on the United States because it is the United States of America, which is a beacon of hope and liberty, with all of our imperfections, because it is the defender of freedom around the world.

We are challenged now, as we were never challenged before, to tell the world what we believe in. What do we stand for? The sanctity of human life, the dignity of man—we stand for these principles, and we shall fight for them, if necessary. And we shall prevail, with God's help, and we shall discover that no enemy can destroy this people. No adversary can weaken our resolve. And that the faith and the hope of the Jewish people are woven into the very pattern, the very fabric of Western civilization, and that hope and that faith will be greater and stronger than all the forces of evil.

That is our message. I would like to share with you an image that was brought to my attention by a colleague who was part of the group mission that visited Israel recently. He describes a memorial service that was held at the site of the Dolphinarium. That is the place where a group of twenty teenage kids were killed by a terrorist bomb. Someone had erected a makeshift memorial. It was a sculpture of a young girl. She was dancing. And the simple sculpture bore a simple inscription which reads, "We will not stop dancing."

That is my message on these Days of Awe. Do not stop dancing. We may have a difficult year in Israel and in America, but we must not, we dare not, stop dancing. If we do, the enemy wins.

We are part of the two most wonderful peoples in the history of the world. I am so proud to belong to both of these wonderful peoples. At this critical juncture, at this moment of truth, I am proud to be a Jew; I am proud to be an American.

God bless America. God bless the State of Israel. God bless us all.

The Miracle of Dialogue

Jewish folklore tells of a little boy who sat with his grandfather in the synagogue on Yom Kippur. The grandfather was not certain that the child was reciting his prayers properly, and he turned to him and in a rather stern manner said in Yiddish, "Hecher, hecher"—"Louder, louder." At that point the boy looked up and said, "Am I talking to you?"

Prayer can be experienced in many ways. But the most satisfying prayer is, in Martin Buber's words, a dialogue between "I" and "Thou," an exalted conversation between man and God. A Polish Hasidic rebbe who used a telephone in Warsaw for the first time answered a disciple who asked what he had learned from the new invention, "What I say *here* is answered *there*."

This divine-human dialogue is the fulfillment of the promise that God made to His prophet Isaiah in a celebrated verse: "Lechu na v'ni-vachecha, yomar ha-shem"—"Come now, let us reason together; let us talk to each other: even if your sins are as scarlet, they shall be white as snow."

What distinguishes us from the rest of the animal kingdom is the capacity to use language—to speak and interpret, to talk and to listen. Indeed, the power of communication is our greatest source of blessing. On this day, more than any other, it connects us with God. It also presents us with the most serious potential for grievous sin.

There are twelve phrases in the "Al Chet" of Yom Kippur that directly involve the sinful use of language—and most of the other sins involve words as well. "For the sin which we have committed before Thee—with utterance of the lips; by unclean lips; by impure speech; by denying and lying; by scoffing; by slander; by idle gossip; by levity; by talebearing; by vain oaths," and the list continues.

As we recognize the perversion of language, we understand why the lines of authentic communication between God and man and between man and man grow weak and falter and break down. In every waking moment, the sound waves are filled with words to convince, to excite, and to entertain. The mass media bombard our senses with words to persuade, to sell, and to stimulate. What inflation can do to currency can happen as well to language. It can become devalued.

We talk when we have nothing to say, and when we have something to say, we find words inadequate to express our thoughts and feelings. A torrent of language flows over us constantly. We have notes of explanation, memos of discussion, letters of understanding, announcements of information, but, somehow, nothing really helps.

We know that deep within us the need to communicate is intense and urgent. This failure of communication is one of the most disturbing problems we face in our shared lives—in our homes, with our friends, at work, in our country, with Jews in Israel and in other parts of the world.

This breakdown presents us with an irony both bitter and poignant, because one of the great achievements of modern technology has been the revolution in communications. We can be in contact with the most remote places of the world. Pictures can be transmitted instantly by satellite of events from the remote jungles of Africa to the urban centers of the United States. We have assumed that because a person can speak in New York and be heard instantly around the world we have solved, once and for all, the problem of communication. We have not, because every day we discover that although we can transcend the barriers of physical space and geographical distance, there are great barriers of the spirit that still divide us. What we meant to say was not understood; what others wanted to tell us, we failed to perceive.

Several years ago, scientists launched a space probe toward the far-thest reaches of the galaxy. Its purpose was to see whether there was life out there and to communicate with it, if possible. The capsule contained pictures of a man and a woman, mathematical symbols, and a diagram of the position of the earth and our own solar system. Presumably, if there are forms of life in outer space, they will find the capsule, open it, figure out the diagrams, and be moved to send back greetings. It may be that we will open up communication for the first time with other forms of intelligent life beyond our earth. While I am in favor of communication, I was not greatly excited about this effort for two reasons. The first is we can't possibly get a response for at least seventy-five thousand years. No doubt my lack of interest shows a deplorable selfishness.

The second is that the most difficult problems of communication are not with outer space, not with the people of Mars, but with the here and the now, the people who attend the synagogue with us and the people whom we see every day. Real communication is very hard to achieve, and I don't mean the "Good morning . . . Great day we're having" variety that passes for conversation.

Real communication involves a meeting of the minds. It means making one's self understood to another human being, achieving rapport with one's fellow man, breaking down the walls that separate one person from another. This challenge is not being met.

The story is told of a woman in a hospital whose doctor would come daily to visit her. He would check her over quickly and then walk out. She grew very angry at this, and one day she said to him, "You come in every day, give a quick look, never say anything—and then leave. You never even ask me how I feel." He said, "You're right." The next time he visited her, he said, "Well, Mrs. Potofsky, how are you feeling today?" She replied, "Doctor, don't ask!"

I believe that we are approaching, in some ways, the breakdown of human communication in our time.

A contemporary author once pointed out an illusion about communication. She said the more people are reached by mass communication, the less they communicate with each other. The proliferation of one-way messages, whether in print or on the air, seems to have increased rather than lessened the alienation of the individual. With some sarcasm, she writes that friendly, gregarious America is full of intensely lonely people for whom radio and, increasingly, television provide the illusory solace of company.

We pass each other with headphones clamped to our ears. We call talk shows in the hope that someone will listen to us. We flock to singles' bars, and we place ads in papers, searching for someone to share our most intimate feelings.

I observe this painful aspect of contemporary life in many settings. Men and women of different races, religions, creeds, and social backgrounds can live side by side for years and never know one another. Neighbors may be not merely strangers but enemies. This is true not only in an individual country or across national boundaries, but it may also be true in the most personal and sensitive of relationships.

When dialogue ceases, love dies, and resentment and hate are formed. People who enter a rabbi's study, who are anguished and burdened, generally have a problem which can be reduced in its essential dimension to the catch phrase of "a breakdown in communication." If they could communicate with each other, they wouldn't need to seek the counsel of a third party. Husbands and wives can lose the power to share the meaning of their lives. They cannot speak to one another in any language, whether the language of words or of deeds, and consequently they drift apart. That is typically the beginning of the end of a marriage.

Sometimes parents are unable to reach their children. A mother once cried out to me, and it's a familiar lament, "I never feel that my children hear what I'm really saying." And do you know what young people say? They express the same frustration about their parents.

How do we deal with the issue of communication? How do we respond to God's challenge? How do we revitalize the process of dialogue?

The first principle that we must always remember is the most difficult. We are black or white or Jew or Christian or Democrat or

Communist or parent or child, but each of us is more than a label. Each of us is unique. Each of us has his or her own tradition, environment, and situation, with his own feelings and perceptions; with his own fears and desires; with his own ancestral wounds, inflections, accents, and style. If you wish to reach me, you must make the effort to understand me in all my unique individuality. Recognize, appreciate, and accept the sorrow and the pride, the hope and the fear, which form the substance of my character.

Don't make me over in your image, for it is not greater or more noble than the image of God in which I was created. Speak to me and I'll listen, but only if you address the real me, the one who is unique. Don't talk to me as though I am an average person, a statistic, or an extension of a computer program. Whatever truth or right or faith you seek to express in advance, put my personal name and my address on it. Know who I am. Know where I live. These are the only name and address I have, and the person who changes his name or address does so very rarely and quite reluctantly.

A six year old became separated from his mother in a crowded supermarket and began shouting frantically, "Mary! Mary!" That was the mother's name, and she came running. "Son," she said, "you shouldn't call me Mary. I'm Mother to you." "Yes, I know," said the lad, "but this store is full of mothers, and I want mine."

How does God speak to us? How does God speak to a person? How is the conversation recorded in the Bible of a divine revelation? God speaks one by one, out of our individual conscience and our special situation, to our particular need. He begins by calling a name. He says, "Avraham"; he says, "Moshe." God begins with the individual and his uniqueness. Dialogue begins when the person addressed is taken seriously.

The second principle is that communication requires sincerity. It is only sincerity and truthfulness that can repair the broken lines between God and man. The Hebrew proverb puts it this way: "Devarim hayotzim min ha-lev nichnosim el ha-lev"—"Words that come from the heart enter the heart."

What is sincerity? It is the opposite of hypocrisy, deceit, and pretense. To speak sincerely means to speak for truth and right and justice as we see them because they are true and right and not because of the advantage that accrues to us. When you speak to me, I cannot help but ask, "Whose good do you seek?" If the suspicion dawns that you are in quest of your own glory or power, is it any wonder that I close my ears and my heart to what you have to say?

I recall an old story of a farm journal that contained a personal advertisement of a man who wrote, "I am fifty-eight years old. I would like to marry a young woman of thirty who has a tractor. Please send a picture of the tractor."

Finally, to share in dialogue means to speak and listen with empathy, to experience the other side, to feel an event from the side of one's partner in dialogue as well as from one's own side. We do that when we listen carefully, when we listen attentively, when we listen with our whole being.

A high school class in music appreciation was asked the difference between listening and hearing. Finally, a hand went up, and a youngster offered this wise definition: "Listening is wanting to hear."

Many of us are like the little boy depicted in a cartoon I saw the other day. It showed a little fellow talking to his teacher while he is handing her his report card. The caption reads, "I don't want to scare you, Teacher, but my daddy says if I don't get better grades, somebody's gonna get spanked!"

The young man obviously did not get the message his father had addressed to him. He thought it was meant for his teacher. The truth is that the little child in us never quite leaves us. Whenever duties or obligations are spelled out, some people prefer to think that they are not addressed to them but to some other recipient. We need to listen with understanding, for the messages are addressed to us.

When our children tell us their troubles or proudly share their joys, do we really listen? Do we hear the loneliness of the elderly through their talk or through their silence? Do we listen with understanding only when those of our generation speak? Do we help the young to hear the voice of the aged, to hear the sustaining melody that conveys eternal truths?

I received a letter from a black man whom I know only through his correspondence. He wrote to me about the chasm created by racial bitterness and dangerous bigotry. And he said, "I wish to let you know that the hope for forever closing that chasm lies within each of our hearts and minds. Let this letter be my quiet way of extending my hand to you. Let it join with yours and others so that we may form a bond which is strong and resilient."

It is in that spirit that I say we should reaffirm our shared goal with blacks and other minorities to create an open, pluralistic, and just society. Each side has a perspective to give to the other if we can talk and listen to each other with sincerity and respect. Of course we have differences. But we can understand and confront our differences in an atmosphere of friendship. We can become a mighty force on behalf of freedom and justice and opportunity for all Americans.

We think of Israel during the course of this summer. Israel went through the ordeal of an election that resulted in no clear victory for either of the major parties. The differences between the labor alignment and the Likud were not resolved by a decisive vote or a clear mandate. Meanwhile, the tensions between Sephardic and Ashkenazi Jews continue to divide Israeli society. The revelation of a Jewish terrorist underground that consists primarily of religious Jews has added to the woes of the country.

We commend the political leaders of the major parties of Israel, Yitzchak Shamir and Shimon Peres, who have joined forces in a unity government sharing political power. They have affirmed the strength of reason and responsibility as they set about implementing a coalition that can create a new dimension for Israeli society.

And so, on this day of Yom Kippur, God says to each of us, "Come, let us talk to one another." If I seek to hear the word of God, I must come before Him in sincerity and in truth saying, "Not my will be done, but Thy will be done." If we can restore the relationship of trust and confidence both in our public and in our private lives, our words will not be a source of sin but of moral excellence. Our words will not divide us, but they will unite us. They will bind us together as one people, sharing a common dream, moved by a common faith.

The Bible tells us, "The word is not in heaven that we should ask, 'Who will go up there on our behalf and bring it down?' Nor is it across the sea so that it requires a special voyage to retrieve and return it to us, but the word is very close in our hearts and in our mouths."

We have the power to replace hate with love, conflict with understanding, and suspicion with trust. We can overcome the barriers that divide us.

In speaking and listening with sincerity and truth, with honesty and care, we can make the miracle of dialogue happen here and now.

The Pursuit of Happiness

A friend of mine told me the following story. He said, "Our son came home from college for the weekend, and I asked him, 'How are things going?' And he said, 'Good.' And I said, 'How is the food?' And he said, 'Good.' 'And the dormitory?' And he said, 'Good.' And I said, 'They have always had a strong football team. How do you think they will do this year?' And he said, 'Good.' And I said, 'How are your studies going?' And he said, 'Good.' And I said, 'Have you decided on your major yet?' And he said, 'Yes.' And I said, 'What is it?' And he said, 'Communications.'"

There is a great deal of communication that takes place during the course of these High Holidays. Prayers that come from our hearts, yearnings, aspirations, hopes—and we feel, we sense, we hope that God's presence hears our prayers.

The High Holiday liturgy is saturated with prayers of extraordinary beauty. One of the most touching is found in the Amidah: "Remember us unto life, oh king who delightest in life; inscribe us in the Book of Life for Thy sake, oh king of life."

This articulation of our deepest yearning flows naturally from the human heart. The world is beautiful, and it is good to be alive.

But even as we ask for continued life, a haunting question lurks in the background. Are we willing to accept life on any terms? Are there not conditions which would make life too burdensome, too intolerable? Is mere survival enough?

No, we want more than another year of life, as our Rosh Hashanah greetings indicate. We wish each other a "Shanah Tovah"—a happy New Year, a good year. We all desire a particular quality of life, a combination of interest, zest, excitement, achievement, and peace of mind. We want a life that is full and rich in satisfaction. In short, we are praying for a happy life. But what is happiness? What can we ourselves do to achieve it?

Let me state some observations. I do not believe that God can give us happiness. God can provide us with many blessings, but whether they bring happiness depends very largely on us. Happiness is not a gift, it is an achievement.

Americans should be the happiest people in the world. We are the envy of all other nations. But in a mental health survey of recent years only 20 percent of the people who were interviewed said they enjoyed life and were happy.

We encounter paradoxes as we examine the ideal of happiness. We find that those who have every reason to be happy often are not and those whom we consider to be the least likely candidates for happiness have found it.

Every person has his or her "peckel tzores," or "care package." However, despite these inevitable vicissitudes and frustrations, there are many human beings who find life happy and satisfying. Are they the recipients of some run of good fortune not granted to the rest of us? Closer examination reveals that happy people are not always the lucky folk. Many of them have been the victims of the toughest contingencies of life. We can't help but wonder how these people manage to remain cheerful and bright.

A few years ago, a writer pointed out, "If you have a happy life, it is not because you found it that way; it is because you made it that way." This statement suggests that happiness is self-made, a "do-it-yourself" project. If that be true, then the question is, How do we create happiness?

Before we try to discover what happiness is and how it may be achieved, let me briefly indicate what I consider the source of widespread frustration and unhappiness. We have been promised too much, and we have become addicted to such promises even though they could not be fulfilled. We have been advised that we can learn how to love; and become beautiful; and succeed through self-assertion; and negotiate everything; and live out the wildest fantasies, simply by following ten rules, or six steps, or spending a week in LaCosta, or taking a course in self-development. There is a part of us that deeply wants to believe in this fulfillment and falls prey to its seductive appeal.

As long as we believe that the way to personal happiness is through the satiation of every desire, we shall be trapped in a fruitless quest for impossible satisfaction. Anyone who declares, "I want it all" will meet with frustration, disappointment, and resentment.

One of the most tragic sentences in all of literature, says Joshua Liebman, is this: "And they lived happily ever after." "It is tragic because it tells a falsehood about life and it has led countless generations of people to expect something from human existence which is not possible on this fragile, failing, imperfect earth."

It is sometimes hard for us to acknowledge this, but we still want fairy tales to come true. We wish for life to be easy, and we wish for life to be fair, and we wish to be taken care of, and we wish to be perfect, and we wish for our life to be conflict free, and we wish for things to be as we want them to be.

The Declaration of Independence is one of the greatest human documents ever written, but it does contain one misleading phrase—"the pursuit of happiness." It gives the impression that happiness must be pursued and therefore, if pursued, can be captured. Neither is true. Happiness is a by-product, something you achieve while you are altogether intent upon doing something else. The moment you start concentrating on happiness, it fades away. The intense pursuit of happiness is one of the chief sources of unhappiness.

Serious thinkers have not always looked with favor on the phrase "the pursuit of happiness." Not that there is anything wrong with being happy, but they have two reservations. First, is happiness really the highest goal set before humanity? Is it subordinate to or more important than, let us say, the ideal of duty or freedom or honor? And second, can happiness really be acquired by pursuing it? Is it not really a rather elusive prize which you can win only indirectly by living in a certain way and not by relentless chase?

But these debates are academic. Today, we accept happiness as terribly important, and for most, it is the highest value that life has to offer. We no longer ask questions about the wisdom of pursuing it in order to attain it. We do not simply pursue it; we are relentless, fanatic, single minded in our hot chase after it.

I would not want to be cast in the role of the grim-lipped deadly moralist. I find nothing wrong with a life that provides for entertainment, for fun, or for escape provided that these do not contradict the other values that impart excellence to human existence.

My concern, however, is with the great number of Americans who have transformed fun to a way of life, from a casual distraction to a consuming passion, from an occasional release to a total immersion in escape from the challenges to which life summons us all. Perhaps life in this complicated, dangerous, complex, troublesome world is too deadly dull for most people. But still, that is no excuse for avoiding its problems or withdrawing from its demands.

A sage of the Talmud, Ben Zoma, once identified the qualities which comprise happiness. His definition speaks to modern man with as much cogency as it did to our forebears some two thousand years ago. "Who is wealthy? He who rejoices in his portion."

The first element that enters the equation is wealth. It may seem strange that a teacher who represents a religious tradition speaks in material terms. But the Jewish tradition is not naive or unrealistic. Poverty and happiness are not faithful companions. There are millions of people in underprivileged countries around the world who would define happiness as a loaf of bread, a bowl of rice, a thatched roof, or steady and secure employment. Abject poverty and heartrending needs lead to a life of despair and bareness. Who is wealthy? He who rejoices in his lot and is grateful for it. Ben Zoma grasped the essential truth about the human heart. Our needs are few, our wants limitless. If we live tormented by limitless wants and desires, we shall never know satisfaction; we shall never have contentment. The only way to achieve this is to control desire, to look upon the blessings one enjoys in today's world with gratitude, recognizing that they are far more than our forebears ever had.

Ben Zoma asks, "Who is the person of power?" The sages knew of great conquerors. They encountered the mighty emperors of Rome, but they did not conceive of them as men of power because they saw that they were driven by ruthless ambition and consuming lust which were ultimately self-destructive. So, the rabbis turned their gaze inward, declaring that true power is in self-mastery. "Who is a strong man?" "He who conquers himself." What the sages say to contemporary man is "Conquer your anger. Conquer your despair." Those who seek to dominate others are often victims of inner insecurity and constant weakness. The art of self-control is the greatest and most enduring form of strength.

"Who is the wise man?" Wisdom was the central quest of the sages. Who is wise? She who has mastered the law? She who has uncovered the mysteries of the universe? She who has studied the words of the scholars? This was not the answer of Ben Zoma. "Who is a wise person? She who learns from everyone." A truly wise person has an unclosed mind, a mind receptive to new ideas that can extract from human experience a rich source for understanding and insight. Wisdom is not restricted to the classroom or the university lecture hall. Wisdom is the ability to respond to the stimulation of life's experiences. If we can listen with understanding to the words of children, to the insights of the aged, to the sayings of the common folk, we can acquire new perspectives on our sometimes too familiar world. To be truly educated means to be open to new challenges of thought all the time.

There is one more factor in this equation of happiness. "Who is honored? She who honors others." The person worthy of honor looks upon humanity with deference and thoughtfulness. Attaining a position of power or a position of wealth and success is no guarantee that a person will be honored. But if we can respond to another human being with respect, if we can see in him a unique individuality stamped by that same divine power that makes life incalculably precious, then we shall create a climate in which honor and respect can flourish and grow.

Ben Zoma has given us guidelines for the acquisition of happiness. They are simply stated, but their implementation requires limitless patience, concern, and understanding. Ben Zoma not only told us what happiness is, he also told us what happiness is not. Happiness is not in a pill, or a bottle, or a distant land, or some contrived amusement. Happiness is, as God's Law described in the Bible, "not far away in heaven, but in your heart." Seek the happiness that lies ahead. May your search be crowned with success.

The New Narcissism

According to Jewish tradition, the High Holidays are dedicated to Heshbon Hanefesh, "the stock-taking of the soul." It is during this period that we have an opportunity to contemplate our lives, to consider our errors, to repent of our sins, and to make plans to reorder the pattern of our existence. On this Kol Nidre night, I wish to discuss a sad phenomenon of our time, a widespread attitude that, I believe, has had a pernicious impact on the lives of many and that has generated moral confusion and spiritual decline. This is not an easy subject to discuss, and indeed, some may take offense at some of the views that will be expressed. Someone once defined a diplomat as a person "who thinks twice and then says nothing." I have thought about this theme many times, and I shall endeavor to define my concern, share my dismay, and propose those affirmations which the Jewish tradition embodies.

Since this subject is not easily defined without reference to psychological terms and theological concepts, I choose to begin my presentation with a poem that provides, in its clarity, what it lacks in elegance.

There was an old man who prayed:

> Lord, bless me and my wife,
> My son, John, and his wife,
> Us four and no more.

55

Further down the street there lived a childless couple whose prayer was shorter and narrower.

> Lord, bless us two,
> And that will do.

Around the corner lived a bachelor who prayed:

> Lord, bless only me.
> That's as far as I can see.

My topic has now been introduced. I am referring to the moral weakness of selfishness, of egocentrism. I am focusing our attention on the person who is interested exclusively in himself, who is bent on taking pleasure and incapable of giving any, who judges all people and all things by their usefulness to him.

I am concerned about a form of self-love so intense, so constant, and so limiting that all relationships are reduced to the question, What am I getting out of it? This psychological phenomenon has a name. It is called narcissism.

The name comes from a legend of the ancient Greeks. Narcissus was a handsome youth and very proud of his own beauty. Many girls loved him, but he paid no attention to them. The nymph Echo was so hurt by his coldness that all but her voice faded away.

Narcissus was punished. He fell in love with his own reflection in a pool of clear water. He was so much in love with himself that he could not leave the pool until he died.

Articles, essays, and books in the last year are pointing to an increasingly prevalent strain in our culture which is called "the new narcissism." A great many psychological cults and quasi-religious movements demonstrate this obsession with self. Selfishness and moral insensitivity now assert themselves in the general culture as enlightenment and psychic excellence. This emerging worldview centers solely on the self, with individual pleasure as its highest good. Those who follow this ideal insulate themselves in a cocoon of self-absorbed rapture and find meaning in self-indulgence.

We used to think of idolatry as the worship of images of wood or stone, an ancient practice restricted to the primitive and unsophisticated. Modern man has discovered a new form of idolatry. It is the idolization, the deification, of the isolated self. One observer described this period as the "me" decade. Another says that the insignia of this movement could be the single letter "I" on a blank white background. Are we becoming "the selfish generation?"

Let me cite a few signs of the times.

A recent article in *Newsweek*, "Getting Your Head Together," describes the experience of a fifty-two-year-old mother of three in Bethesda, Maryland, who has undergone an emotional odyssey involving the new "therapies." She has experienced transactional analysis, primal scream, bioenergetics, yoga, guided fantasy, Arica, nude marathon, Gestalt therapy, psychosynthesis, and most recently EST. With each new probe of her mind she claims, "I discover a different part of me. My life is an adventure now—it keeps getting better and better and better."

A Detroit newspaper asked in the Sound Off column, "Are you disillusioned by parenthood?" The question was triggered by Ann Landers quoting a survey that showed 70 percent of parents would not have children if they had to do it over again. The answers were revealing. While 60 percent said they were not disillusioned, 40 percent agreed that they were disillusioned. Children are seen, by this group, as a joyless burden, an unwelcome obligation that prevents the fullest enjoyment of life's pleasures.

A recent book, *The Mistress Condition*, written by Catherine Breslin, describes a new kind of woman, the mistress of her own affairs, self-sufficient, uncommitted, responsible only to herself. She writes, "I have never had a husband, a child, or an abortion; never had a boss, a 9–5 job, or a pension plan. I have no life insurance and several lovers."

Another item. We are now indoctrinating our young at an early age into the values and practices of narcissism. According to a recent article in a Detroit newspaper, there is now a hair- coloring expert who offers services to seven-, eight-, and nine-year-old girls who learn how to improve upon nature. (Remember, Narcissus was completely and utterly fascinated by gazing at his own image.) Why wait for adulthood for narcissistic pleasure when it is available at the age of seven?

As a rabbi, I find a painful condition affecting a significant number of people in their middle years—the frustration of would-be grandparents. When these individuals realize that their married children don't want children they suffer an ache, a hidden hurt, an emptiness. One man recently expressed his frustration to me: "Isn't that part of the dream of having your own children, that someday they'll have children?"

Of course, there is a cost in raising a child—financial, physical, and emotional. In a hedonistic society, the cost seems too high. Children do not fit into future plans and the fulfillment of self-realization. They limit or modify the values of personal freedom, comfort, travel, and career goals.

But the ache, the void, and the longing remain. The generations cannot speak to each other about this concern, so sensitive and painful is the subject.

The increasing rate of divorce is related to the injurious effect of narcissism on the institution of marriage. Within one's immediate circle of friends and acquaintances, I would wager that there is at least one separation and divorce that occurred recently in which either partner (or both) cast aside responsibilities to young children or to other people in their declared intent to find happiness; fulfillment; or simply a new, exciting alternative to a marriage that seemed routine and dull.

We know that a loveless marriage that produces frustration and misery cannot long endure. But some of us, influenced by a pleasure-seeking and self-obsessed culture, have made impossible demands of marriage, have unrealistic expectations of marriage. To live in the relationship of marriage and a family means to have the capacity to live with a measure of frustration. Human relationships of depth and meaning require time, energy, some sacrifice, and generosity of soul. All these embody the opposite of instant gratification and continuous self-indulgence.

It was Hillel, the great sage of the Jewish people, who declared, "lm ain anl il, ml il?"—"If I am not for myself, who will be for me?" Our own health, education, security, and achievement are natural and proper personal priorities. We have both a right and a responsibility to strive for the highest of which we are capable, to reach out for worthy goals, to succeed and to excel and to fulfill our dreams and realize our ambitions.

But if anyone seeks his own happiness and fulfillment in isolation from the world in which he lives, he will never find them. We are becoming a society of separate selves, a culture of atomized, nuclear people, many of whom are in search of some new form of consciousness, some new philosophy, some new cult in which the self and its sensations, its pleasures, and its demands replace family, friends, tradition, or even God.

When I was in Charlevoix this summer, I saw a drive-in church. This new aberration, which is becoming ever more popular, started, like many other strange movements, in California and is now moving east. The drive-in church has two advantages. One is that you don't have to dress up or shave because no one will see you. And the other is that you don't have to face anyone. You can recite the service, pray to God, and then leave without becoming involved with the rest of the congregation, without entering into a face-to-face encounter with any other worshiper, and that seems to be an attraction in our narcissistic time.

You can hear this development in the new language. The code word today is *liberated*. The liberated student, the liberated woman, the liberated man. Liberated from what? From obligations, from the routines of daily life, from the constraints and the disciplines that enable human relationships to endure. The liberated are those who have successfully rejected traditions, loyalties, and obligations.

Abraham Heschel once pointed out that the question of modern man is, What will I get out of life? What escapes his attention are fundamental but forgotten questions. What will life get out of me? What will society get out of me? Modern man believes the world is indebted to him. But our tradition teaches that basic to man's existence is his indebtedness to society and to God.

The distinguishing characteristic of the narcissist is that he or she never truly matures, never grows up, but sees the world as a child, as an extension of his own need and desire. In our society, there is no need to become an adult. One may remain a child forever. It is possible to encounter those who have acquired a good education, a professional job, and a fine standard of living and yet remain as adult children. In medieval paintings, children look like miniature adults. In some tableaus from life today, adults appear as wrinkled adolescents.

Judaism has rejected the idolatries of every age. It has heroically exposed the false gods and torn down the graven images. What healing message issues from the depths of that wise and humane tradition which preserves for us as it did for all the generations a sacred vision of man?

First, we are summoned to remember Hillel's complementary statement and directive: "V'ca-asher ani l'atzmi, ma ani?"—"If I am for myself alone, what good am I?" A person all wrapped up in himself makes a very small package and, paradoxically, a very heavy one to carry.

Life becomes most worthwhile when it is filled with concern as wide as the whole world and as far-reaching as eternity. John Mason Brown once said, "What happiness is, no person can say for another. But no one, I am convinced, can be happy who lives only for himself. The joy of living comes from immersion in something that we know to be bigger, better, more enduring and worthier than we are."

We may formulate the Jewish response to the cult of narcissism with three words that carry a precious freightage of idealism and faith—*caring, commitment,* and *community.*

Caring. A noted musician once said, "I feel the capacity to care is the thing which gives life its deepest significance." Of course people care. There could not be any synagogues if people did not care. There would not be institutions of learning and culture if people did not care. Support for Israel and world Jewry would not be provided unless Jews cared. Nothing good in our community could exist if there were not people who choose every day of their lives to care. Our tradition teaches that the measure of a man is reflected in how much he cares and about what he cares. Through caring for others, by serving them, a person lives meaningfully.

In caring for others, in helping them grow, I discover my own distinctive powers. The writer grows caring for his ideas. The teacher grows caring for his students. The parent grows caring for his child.

Those who care do not say "no" to causes which beg for volunteers and help. Those who care do not shut their eyes to human need. Those who care are not perennial seekers after diversion and recreation and escape. Those who care discover the joy of knowing they are needed and learning how to serve.

Commitment. In the confused culture of today, which offers us too many alternatives, so many options, we need to reaffirm the power of commitment—the commitment to marriage, the commitment to children, the commitment to integrity and faithfulness, the commitment to the future, the commitment to faith.

Every commitment imposes responsibilities that are often unforeseeable, periodically frustrating, and occasionally baffling. But it is in precisely these things that we undergo the process of human development, that we are challenged to progress and to mature.

At the center of our consciousness is our commitment to being Jews. However tenuous our loyalties at other times, how tentative our allegiance, however vague our sense of Jewish piety, on Kol Nidre night we feel the pull of that mysterious force which uplifts us as Jews. We should seek and find within our tradition the meaning that some have been seeking in the substitute faiths of our time. Eight hundred thousand people in this country who have become followers of transcendental meditation spend twenty minutes twice a day meditating, concentrating on their mantras. Among them are many fellow Jews. How I long for the devotion and spiritual capacity of these brethren. If they would renew their commitment to Judaism and offer forty minutes a day to worship, to an encounter with their faith, their lives would be elevated and their heritage revitalized.

Morally, spiritually, and emotionally, our generation needs the synagogue more than any other. In a world where so many of the authentic values are being mocked, we need the reassurance which the synagogue can give us. At a time when there is so much cynicism, we need to restore our belief in goodness and truth and justice. In a world where so much conspires to diminish our humanity, we need the restorative healing which the synagogue provides. In renewing our commitment to Jewish practice and faith, we should avail ourselves of those great resources which nurture our soul and sustain our spirit.

Community. The overwhelming majority of our prayers are not in the singular but the plural. "Our God, God of our ancestors." Each of us comes before God not as a separate person but as a member of a great, extended family. The whole people of Israel are included in the orbit of our concern. Ours is not an "I-Thou relationship," as Buber described it, but rather a "We-Thou relationship." We don't say to God on this day, "Hear me," but "Hear us." Not "Answer me," but "Answer us."

Elie Weisel once remarked that alone, a Jew is nothing. But if he is with other Jews, he is a force, because then automatically he inherits all the strength and all the tears, all the sorrows and all the joys of his ancestors. The Jew alone cannot be Jewish. A Jew must belong to a community.

There is a great Yiddish dictionary that is being published now, although only the first volume has been finished. The author, Yudel Mark, collected all the folk sayings that surround each word that he defines. One notes a whole column on the word *Adam*, "man." One of the definitions is this: *Adam* is an abbreviation. It stands for "ich, du, mir"—"I, you, us." That is the shortest and simplest Jewish definition of what it means to be a mentsch: Ich, du, mir.

As a Jew, I know that my life is intimately connected with the destiny of my people, the fate of Israel, the strength of the Jewish community. I die a little if I deny their claim upon me and my loyalty to them.

Rooted in the soil of my people, I draw strength, sustenance, and meaning.

We, as Jews, can teach our fellow Americans about the meaning of community. For what this country needs now is a greater awareness of our interdependence, of our self-understanding as Americans that we belong to a national community in which we care for our land, in which we are prepared to make commitments to our country, in which we assume responsibility for her welfare.

Karle Baker, in a poem called "Pronouns," summarized our theme.

> The Lord said,
> "Say, 'We'";
> But I shook my head,
> Hid my hands tight behind my back, and said,
> Stubbornly,
> "I."

> The Lord said,
> "Say, 'We'";
> But I looked upon them, grimy and all awry,
> Myself in all those twisted shapes? Ah, no!
> Distastefully I turned my head away,
> Persisting,
> "They."

> The Lord said,
> "Say, 'We'";
> And I
> At last
> Richer by a horde
> Of years
> And tears,
> Looked in their eyes and found the heavy word
> That bent my neck and bowed my head;

Like a shamed schoolboy then I mumbled low
"We, Lord."

May God grant to all who need these gifts the wisdom and the strength to grow beyond "I" to "we," beyond narcissism to caring, beyond cynicism to commitment, beyond self to community.

FAITH

What is faith? It is the ability to feel the touch of a hand made cold by death, to hear across the great barrier the gentle, soothing voice of those we loved. It is the ability to face the trials of life with courage and to confront its problems with undimmed eyes.

—RABBI HARRY HALPERN

We believe that God is just and to Him the great and small are alike. We believe He is a righteous Judge.

—V'HOL MA-AMINIM,
prayer book

The Missing Piece

At the end of June, I sustained a mild stroke requiring hospitalization and a subsequent period of convalescence. A passage in *The Ethics of the Fathers* came to my mind: "From all my teachers have I gathered wisdom." I have learned, or perhaps more accurately, I have relearned, certain truths as a consequence of my illness.

First, I have a renewed sense of wonder as I contemplate the functions of the human body.

How wise were our sages who determined that even before we begin the morning prayers, we offer a special blessing recognizing with gratitude the way our bodies are fashioned with passages and vessels, so that if one of these be opened or closed improperly, it would be impossible to exist and stand before Thee, the Father of humanity. One has a renewed appreciation for the complexity and the efficiency of the human body as a consequence of these experiences.

One can declare that the functions of the body are a daily miracle. When sickness or malfunction occurs, the healing of the body is no less the product of miracles.

A colleague told me the story of a rabbi who took ill and was hospitalized. The Board of Trustees of his congregation composed a resolution calling for a full and speedy recovery for the rabbi. The vote was

20–4. When I told the story to my wife, Leypsa, she didn't laugh. Instead she said, "Who were the four?"

My own experience was the complete opposite of what I just described. Words are not adequate to express my profound appreciation to the people of my congregation during the time of my illness. I was flooded, moved, touched, uplifted by the multitude of cards, telephone calls, messages, contributions, flowers and personal gifts, words of encouragement, and fervent prayers offered on my behalf.

I sensed the transformation of traditional roles as a consequence of my illness. The rabbi is a caregiver. That is his mission. He seeks to help his people by conveying to them faith in God and trust in His wisdom. The rabbi seeks to elicit from his people patience and courage and a spirit of resilience. But because I was ill, the congregation became my caregiver, my collective rabbi, and said to me, in so many words, be strong, be hopeful, be resolute. This was a remarkable experience— one Jew and so many rabbis.

I awoke in a hospital bed the day after the stroke, and then I took an inventory of my assets.

I could see, I could hear, I could touch and feel, I could think, I could talk, I could remember, I could hope, I could pray and sing, I could laugh and cry.

True, I could not then walk without assistance, but that was a temporary deficiency. In time, I was assured, I would walk again.

God had continued to give me an incredible treasury of assets and blessings. In the language of the prayer book, "We thank You for our lives which are in Your hand; for our souls, which are in Your care; for Your miracles, which are daily with us; and for Your wondrous kindness at every moment—morning, noon, and night."

And yet, as the days passed and the physical therapy proceeded, I thought more deeply about what happened to me. Could I find meaning in my illness? Was there a lesson that I should learn from what happened? What if the roles were reversed, what would I say to a friend lying in a hospital bed? And then I remembered a children's fable that adults can appreciate. It was a book by Shel Silverstein entitled *The Missing Piece.*

This children's fable is about a circle that was missing a piece and was very unhappy. This is actually a story about the nature of quest and fulfillment. The circle went everywhere looking for its missing piece— up mountains and down into valleys, through rain and snow and blistering sun. Wherever it went, because it was missing a piece, it had to go very slowly. So, as it went along, it stopped to look at the flowers and talk to the butterflies. Sometimes it sang. It stopped to rest in the cool grass. And wherever it went, it kept looking for its missing piece.

But it couldn't find it. Some pieces were too big, some were too small, some were too square, and some were too pointed. Then, suddenly one day, it found a piece that seemed to fit. The circle was whole again; nothing was missing. It took the piece into itself and started to roll away.

And now, because it was a whole, unbroken circle, it could roll much faster. So, it rolled quickly through the world, past the lakes and past the forests—too fast to get a good look at them. It rolled too quickly to notice the flowers, too fast for any of the butterflies to fly by.

When the wheel realized that it was rolling too fast to do any of the things that it had been doing for years, it stopped and reluctantly put down its missing piece, and it rolled slowly away, heading out into the world, continuing to look for its missing piece.

Now, that is such a beautiful story, I almost don't want to violate its poignancy by taking it apart and trying to understand it. But it is saying some important things. The most important truth is that in a strange and mysterious way which we cannot really understand, a person is more whole when he is incomplete, when he is missing something. That little bit of incompleteness cures him of a delusion of self-sufficiency, opens him up—as it did the circle in the story—to feeling more, seeing more, experiencing more.

In a paradoxical way, the person who has everything will never have some of the most beautiful experiences in life. The person who has everything will never know what it feels like to yearn, to hope. He will never understand the songs and the poetry and the music which are born out of longing, out of grieving, out of incompleteness. You can never make him happy by giving him something he would enjoy because, by definition, he already has it. In a strange way, the person who has everything, who is missing absolutely nothing, is a very impoverished person indeed.

The biblical text that speaks to us is the story of the ancestor of the Jewish people, Jacob, our father, who wrestled one dark night with a hostile angel, the angel of despair. You may remember the story. He received a blessing at the break of dawn, before the coming of the light. At the same time that he was blessed in that struggle, a hip socket was wrenched at the thigh muscle of Jacob. From that time onward, Jacob would always walk with a limp. He would always carry on his flesh the impact of that strange and fateful encounter. And Jacob was told, "Your name shall no longer be Yaakov, the 'supplanter,' but Yisrael, because you have striven with God and man, with beings divine and human, and you have prevailed. You are a prince of God."

But, notice the paradox of the story. The wound and the blessing, the pain and the promise, the ordeal and the transformation came together. They are inseparable. The following passage is both profound and extraordinary. Jacob arrives "shalem," which means "whole," to the city of Shachem. But Jacob was not whole. He was wounded; he was disabled; a piece of him was missing. But he saw the world and he saw himself in a new way. He had become greater and nobler and wiser. And therefore, he was shalem, he was whole.

We are more complete if we are incomplete. That is the paradoxical truth of the story. We are made more whole by the things we don't have. It's true on many levels. When it comes to giving charity, we become more whole through what we give away. We instinctively understand that the person who can afford to be generous, who can afford it psychologically, not only financially, is a more whole person than the man or woman who is afraid to part with what he has because he is afraid that if he gives something away, he is giving away part of himself. The person who is not afraid to be generous because he is not giving himself away comes across as really more whole.

The Bible tells a story about the prophet Elisha. A man came to Elisha with a present of a loaf of bread and an ear of corn. And the prophet told him, "Distribute it to the entire crowd." The man said, "What? Am I supposed to divide this among a hundred people?" And the prophet told him, "Distribute it to all the people, for the Lord has said, 'It will suffice.'" And he gave it to them, and they ate, and they left some over as the Lord had promised.

Now, this is a nice trick to know when you have unexpected company. But the real point to the story is more appropriate. Each of us has the resources, financial, emotional, spiritual, to help a lot of people, but we don't know how much we have until we start giving them away.

The act of strengthening others makes you even stronger. You never know how rich and full you are until you start sharing yourself with others. The person who has grown comfortable with the fact that he is missing a piece in a sense is more whole than the person who thinks he has to be complete and unbroken.

On this day of Rosh Hashana, what I wish for all Jews is a life of goodness, of blessing, of the fulfillment of all worthy desires. There is a story of thousands of people who came to see a renowned Hasidic rabbi before the High Holidays to ask for his blessing. Among them was a matronly grandmother who stood in line for hours in order to be received in an audience. And finally after many hours, she was allowed to see the revered rabbi. There he sat in all his majestic presence, and he spoke to the woman and asked her, "How are things?" She said, "Thank God." "And how is the health of your family?" And she said, "Thank God." "Does your husband make a living?" And she said, "Thank God." "And how is your health?" "Thank God." The rabbi paused and said, "If this is the case, what are we to pray for?" The grandmother answered, "Rabbi, pray that all of this shall not be taken away from me." And that story, in a sense, describes what all of us wish and what is in our hearts as we assemble in prayer on Rosh Hashana.

But the truth is that none of us is that fortunate indefinitely. In time, something is taken away from each of us. No one is exempt from pain. We encounter frustration and failure. We meet with disharmony and discord. To be human is to live in a world where suffering is the common human lot. How do we respond? Will we react in a negative and defensive way? Will we say, "Why me, oh Lord?" Will we lament our missing piece? Will we descend into the depth of bitterness and resentment and self-pity?

Trouble alone does not bring out our best. Trouble is neutral. It can do almost anything to a person. It can make him hard and cruel; it can plunge his life into despair.

But trouble does that to people who take a negative attitude toward it and let trouble do that to them. There are others who have something in them so creative that their calamity becomes their opportunity.

The forty-eighth chapter of the Book of Isaiah has a remarkable verse. The prophet is chastising his people. Among other things, he says to them, "I purged you, but nothing came of it. I tested you in the furnace, but all in vain." The prophet is saying to the people, "You have been through the furnace of affliction, but you haven't learned anything from the experience." He is saying to them, "What do you have to show for your suffering? The tragedy is not that you have endured pain; the tragedy is that your pain was wasted. You are not wiser or better; you haven't changed." The prophet expected the people to do more than accept trouble. He expected them to use it. That is the challenge. When our eyes are dimmed by tears, there are things we can learn, there are things we can understand, there are things we can grasp.

"I walked a mile with pleasure," the poet wrote. "She chattered all the way, but left me none the wiser, for all she had to say. I walked a mile with sorrow and ne'er a word said she, but oh, the things I learned from her, when sorrow walked with me."

We speak about victims of circumstance. I would like to recognize victors over circumstance—people who use negative experiences to get some new insight into life, some understanding that they never had before. I suggest some of those gifts.

The first is wisdom, and that is the wisdom to know that everybody has a missing piece, that none of us is whole, unblemished, and unscarred. Not all handicaps are physical, and not all the weaknesses are visible, but to be human is to be flawed and imperfect. And things are not necessarily what they seem.

Some of us are burdened by a sense of inferiority and inadequacy. Some of us carry around childhood scars inflicted by constant criticism and bitter rejection. Some of us feel unworthy of being loved—others cannot give love. Some are burdened by guilt; others are filled with rage. Some are battered by fear, others by frustration and failure. Some of us carry heartaches because of our children. Some of us are tormented by our parents. Some of us are consumed by envy and others by greed.

Everyone has a missing piece. I recall an old Italian story. In Naples, there lived a man who could not shake a feeling of deep depression. He went to the doctor for help. After a thorough examination, the physician said to the patient, "There is nothing physically wrong with you. I have a suggestion. Go to the theater tonight. You will hear a great comedian. His name is Carlini. He brings laughter to crowds at every performance. He will drive away your sadness." At these words, the patient burst into tears. "Doctor," he said, "you don't understand. I am Carlini."

It is wisdom to know that we have not been singled out by a malicious fate for special abuse. We are simply paying the price for being human. And before we become too envious of our neighbors and friends and associates who seem to have it all, we might pause to reflect that each of us carries his own shabby secrets and dark sorrows, his own invisible burdens; he too has a missing piece.

Years ago, the renowned actress Helen Hayes suffered the loss of her young and gifted daughter, Mary. And she wrote, "When God afflicts the celebrated of the world, it is His way of saying 'None is privileged in my eyes. All are equal.'" There is a democracy about pain. The missing piece teaches us compassion and awakens in us greater sympathy for other human beings. Because of our own troubles, we understand the burdens of others—their anxieties, their woes, their hurt, their frustrations.

It has been noted repeatedly by observers of the Jewish people that there is a remarkable quality about Jews. They have made such outstanding contributions to the world in healing, in service, and in generosity. Why is this? I believe this is because we haven't forgotten our own persecution, our own enslavement in ancient and modern times. There is a famous verse in the Torah that is repeated fifty times. It is not the Sh'ma. It is not the statement that "you should remember the Lord, our God." No, this verse to which I make reference repeated fifty times says, "Remember you were slaves in the land of Egypt." You were strangers; you were outcasts; you were persecuted. Never forget this, for you should know the heart of the stranger. The experience of slavery could have made the Jew a prisoner of his own bitter memories, could have made him filled with rage in his quest for vengeance. But the reverse happened. Out of his painful memory, the Jew learned compassion for all who suffer—the stranger, the slave, the outcast, and the victim of cruelty. That verse is the basis of Jewish morality.

We need to use our Egypt, not waste it. We must make it a source of inspiration, compassion, caring, and tenderness.

The missing piece can offer us strength. It is not always the victories of life that fortify us. Sometimes the defeats and the disappointments strengthen a person and make him what he is. Many people owe the grandeur of their lives to the tremendous difficulties they faced, to the obstacles they overcame.

This story comes out of the Second World War. The Nazis imprisoned a young man in Latvia who had remarkable talent. He was not Jewish, but he was persecuted by the enemy. He was studying to be a concert pianist. They broke his fingers, and his dream was forever shattered. After the war, he came to the United States and became a physician. Today, he is retired, but he remains the most renowned oncologist in the metropolitan Detroit community.

Some years ago, I found a story that uplifted the hearts of all America. Nine handicapped adventurers captured the headlines. Five of them were blind, two were deaf, one was an epileptic, and the last had an artificial leg. They captured headlines because they climbed Mount

Ranier, which is over fourteen thousand feet, in the state of Washington. After their descent, one of the blind mountain climbers explained the success of the adventure quite simply. He said, "We had a lot of help from each other on the trip." We all have a perilous journey through life. It is an adventure filled with obstacles and pitfalls. Each of us must negotiate it as we are with an assortment of handicaps, because each of us has a missing piece. We can succeed together, but we need a lot of help from one another on the trip.

When we have a missing piece, we yearn for faith. Faith in God is not easily attained when we encounter life's sorrows and pain. It is comparatively easy to say, "The Lord is my shepherd" when He maketh me to lie down in green pastures. It is another matter when I walk through the valley of the shadow of death. How many are capable of saying then, "Thou art with me"? Judaism does not explain evil in the world. It doesn't declare that God created a world of all good and no evil. It says that man is born to trouble as the sparks fly upward.

There are times when I envy doctors. This is a season of confession, and I have to confess. You see, if something goes wrong with you and it is not quite clear what it is, the doctor can tell you "it's a virus," and you will be satisfied. But I visit a man who is lying in a hospital bed. And he says, "Why am I lying here with a broken leg while my brother-in-law, the scoundrel, the rascal, the good-for-nothing, is enjoying a vacation in Hawaii? Why, Rabbi?" I wish I had an answer that would be the equivalent of a virus.

I am like the minister who was sitting next to a fragile elderly lady who was taking her first airplane ride. She was a little nervous, as many people are under those circumstances. As luck would have it, the airplane got into a violent storm. The plane tossed about, and the passengers were greatly affected by the turbulence. The elderly woman became very apprehensive, on the borderline of hysteria, and she turned to the clergyman and said, "Father, you are a man of God. Can't you do something about this?" He said, "Madam, I am in sales, not management."

Too often, what poses as faith is illusion. We believe in God Who is supposed to grant us and our loved ones special immunity and exemption against the ravages of life. Death on the highway can claim others' relatives but not ours. Sickness may invade the bodies of others but not ours. When the hours of anguish strike, we are ready to surrender what we thought was our faith. If we are wise, we will leave behind our illusions and struggle on to a higher faith. It's the faith of the psalmist who said, "Though I am fallen, I shall rise again. Though I dwell in darkness, Thou art my light. When my heart and my strength fail, Thou art my strength and my portion forever." We all know moments when our faith is shaken. Joseph Rosensaft survived Auschwitz and Bergen Belsen. He was once asked by an interviewer of the *New York Times* what he thought about God. And he answered, "I don't want to fight with Him, but a medal He should not expect from me."

It is part of our tradition that throughout our history Jews have challenged God, holding Him responsible for what the world is and how it operates. We argue with God; we confront God. We level charges of injustice against God. But throughout this process, one thing remains clear. We are not denying God. Elie Weisel, the renowned survivor of the horror of the Holocaust, once remarked, "A Jew can be Jewish with God, against God, but not without God." And ironically, this struggle is what confirms our belief.

Faith does not dissolve our sorrow; it does not anesthetize us against pain. It doesn't answer all our questions. But faith shows us a way to go on despite anguish and heartache. Not all the darkness can be dispelled, but there is enough light to live by, to guide us along the way, and we do not walk alone. The God Who created this marvelous universe can be relied upon to give us courage and strength to endure and to prevail.

Every one of us is incomplete in one way or another. We are missing something from our lives whose absence weighs us down, slows us down like the circle in the story, compels us to see everything in our lives in a different way.

There is so much for which we ought to be grateful. It is when our blessings are threatened that we discover how precious they are. I learned that lesson from my own experience, and I learned it from the experiences of my congregation. They have taught me so much. I have intimately known those who have passed through diverse experiences of life, from serene safety out into the raging storms of struggle and suffering. And I have witnessed the growth of the human spirit through these experiences, again and again. I have seen the souls of men and women rise through a life of selfishness and complacency into a life of self-sacrifice and service. And I see beauty and radiance in their faces which were never there before.

So, the missing piece adds a precious dimension of life. May we receive, in the year that has now begun, God's bounty. May we have everything good—good health, good fortune, joy, well-being, love, and fulfillment. But no one is exempt from pain, and no one has made a truce with hardship, and no one has a contract with God. For all who struggle with life's darker side, I submit this prayer: "May you discover how the missing piece offers you precious gifts—wisdom and compassion, strength and faith and gratitude. May you, like Father Jacob, become greater and wiser and more blessed. May you enter the place of your striving as he did, shalem—whole, complete—at peace with yourself, with humanity, and with God."

(Based on an interpretation of Rabbi Harold Kushner)

When Life Is Not Fair

It is at this time that we assemble in anticipation of the Yizkor service, which is dedicated to the memory of those whom we have loved and lost. The service of this year has special meaning, a poignant dimension, for the Groner family.

On March 5, my wife, Leypsa, and I and our two sons, David and Joel, stood at the grave of our daughter and sister, Debbie Groner, and we said our final farewell as we laid her to rest. As the traditional words were recited, questions arose within me—questions that have agitated the hearts of the faithful since the beginning of man's search for God—questions that were asked by me so many times before. Why do the righteous suffer? Why do bad things happen to good people? Why is the world so unfair? Why does the compassionate and just God allow cruelty and injustice to prevail in the world He has created? Where is God in the midst of this suffering and anguish? For me, these became more than philosophical questions and theological formulations when we stood at Debbie's grave. These questions became intensely personal. They touched the very depth of who we are, what we believe, and what strength we can find in our sorrow. The answers that can assuage our pain are to be found with great difficulty, if found at all, in our search for meaning and understanding.

I turn to the teachings of our tradition. The first answer that I find is

Olam Haba, the world to come. There is so much injustice in the world. As an old Yiddish proverb puts it: "God runs the world but not like a mentsch." God is omniscient and omnipotent but seemingly indifferent. There must be another world where everything crooked is put straight, where the suffering of the righteous in this world is measured against an eternity of bliss in the world to come. As a rabbi, I have seen so many people sustained by the belief in another world out there waiting for us, a wonderful, loving, and peaceful world. And they find serenity and peace in that belief. But my consciousness has been shaped by a rationality that challenges this belief. Besides, no one has described the floor plan of heaven, no one has brought us back a report, no one can declare with certainty the nature of this other world. Besides, the Torah and the teachings are about this world, about this life.

I was therefore determined to address this issue and to begin a journey, a quest which would enable me to find those answers that might ease my troubled heart.

I became a rabbi because I committed my life to never giving up searching and yearning for God. I am a rabbi because there is in me, as there is in so many, the belief that we are not alone; that this world is bathed in miracles; and that for every pain there is beauty, for every loss there is love, and for every wound there is wonder.

I continue to seek God because I know this is the human task. I seek, because in that search there is life, and light, and meaning, and even joy. We would like to have our questions answered about how God manages His world. He made some of us too tall, others too short, and most of us deficient in just those things we would like to have. He fashioned some of us in the shape of round pegs and then drove us into square holes. He starves the righteous and feeds the wicked. We would like to know why.

Rabbi Harold Kushner has made the searing remark that the loss of his child has made him a better person, a better rabbi, a wiser and more compassionate counselor—and he would give it all back in an instant if he could have his child back.

We have seen beautiful people, pursuers of truth and kindness, men and women of generosity, living sermons, and yet, they have had to carry burdens of illness, distress, and affliction. As we grow older, we witness the suffering of the good, the death of the all-too-young, and the passing of the righteous. Simultaneously, we see the untroubled lives of the selfish. We know cruel and licentious people who are not scarred by any failure, who are unscathed by any travail, who luxuriate in privilege, and we say life is not fair.

By conventional wisdom, none of this makes sense. We are taught from birth that the good will be rewarded and the evildoer punished. Our service states this belief. As children, when we behaved ourselves and did what our parents told us, if we were not rewarded, at least we were not punished. But if we did the reverse, we soon discovered that punishment would be forthcoming.

When we began to grow up, we gradually became aware that what we had learned as children was not quite so in the marketplace of life, and we recognized the sad truth that life is not fair.

Upon this realization, four responses are possible. First is the answer of submissiveness.

Accept, ask no questions, raise no outcry, seek not to change the scheme of things. The proper mood for living is resignation. As the poet suggested in *The Rubáiyát of Omar Khayyám*, "The Moving Finger writes: and, having writ, moves on: nor all your Piety nor Wit shall lure it back to cancel half a Line, nor all your Tears wash out a Word of it." This is what the Buddhists call "Karma," the wheel of necessity. This is providence, or *bashert*. In the name of fate, the world's unfairness and inequity are tolerated, condoned, and justified.

The second response is bitterness. We can become resentful and succumb to waves of self-pity. We can feel terribly sorry for ourselves. We can hurl our curses at life. We can imitate those of whom it was said, "Like children they are who, when sent to bed, go because they must, but as they climb the stairs, nastily kick each stair by way of angry protest." We have all known such people. I know wives and husbands in broken marriages who, years after the divorce, sometimes decades later, still talk of nothing else than the injustice done them. They become burdens to their friends and family. By preventing themselves from making new lives, they become their own worst enemies. The second response is the lament that life is crooked, justice is not in it. It is proper to be b'ragez—bitter, resentful, angry.

There is a third response—rebellion. The Jewish tradition is reverential of God. It is also *hutzpadik* toward Him. That is why Levi-Yitzchak, on behalf of justice, challenged the God he revered.

The Bible reports three different instances where man challenged God and questioned His justice. Abraham learned of the impending destruction of Sodom and Gomorrah. He reasoned with God, bargained with Him, in order that no question be left regarding the justice of Him who had created the universe. He received an answer that was logical, that made some sense of the divine judgment.

Job was afflicted by misfortune, tragedy, and pain. He protested; he pleaded; he avowed his innocence. After all the answers had been given, God appeared to him in a whirlwind and manifested His spirit unto him.

The third challenge was hurled at God by Jeremiah the prophet. His mood and temper resemble those of contemporary man. He asked, "Wherefore does the way of the wicked prosper? Why are all those that deal treacherously so secure?" God does not put on a cosmic spectacle for Jeremiah. There is no whirlwind for him; no bargain is established; no negotiation is undertaken. He is left to his own resources to contemplate the struggle that awaits him. There is no justification that is issued unto him. The message is blunt: "This is life, Jeremiah. Whatever you face now, there is worse to come. Get used to it, gird your loins, prepare to endure it."

Neither bitterness nor submission is the proper Jewish response. And even rebellion cannot satisfy us. Rebellion will not assuage the pain, or heal the wound, or illumine the darkness.

But, a fourth response is possible. Is life fair? No. Life is decidedly not fair. Life can be grossly, grievously, tragically unfair. But our heritage teaches us that we were put on earth to make it more fair.

Fifty times the Torah reminds us, "We remember you were slaves in the land of Egypt. [Vezacharta Ki Eved Hayita B'eretz Mitzrayim.] You were strangers and outcasts. Never forget this, for you know the heart of the stranger." We remember not to hate; we remember not to submit; we remember not to rebel. We remember to make the world more just.

"Therefore, you shall love the stranger, for you were strangers in the land of Egypt." The experience of slavery could have made the Jew a prisoner of his bitter memories, angry, filled with rage. Life was unfair to him, which could have justified his hatred and revenge. No! From his painful memory, the Jew was to learn compassion for all who suffer, who are strangers, who are slaves, who are victims of cruelty.

Jewish moral teaching states, What is the worst sin? To do unto others what we hate to have done to us, to inflict upon others the unfairness that we have endured. This is the basis of Jewish morality—the more unfair life is, the more fair and just and compassionate we are to be. If life is unfair to you, make it more fair to others. This is therapeutic. This commitment enables us to live in a world which can be unfair—without becoming deranged or filled with bitterness.

Mildred Newman and Bernard Berkowitz, psychotherapists, in *How to Be Your Own Best Friend,* write "People feel very justified in their anger. They can give you all the details of how unfairly they were treated years ago. They usually are right; they did get cheated as children. But what they don't see is they're now cheating themselves. Their rage can't hurt their parents, but it's crippling them. 'It doesn't seem fair. You mean we should just let them get away with it? Wipe the slate clean, after all they put us through? It isn't fair.' But there is nothing you can do about that now. Hamlet tried to even the score and it led to multiple deaths. Life lies in another direction, in letting go, giving up your grievance." But it is more than that. If we make the world more fair, we ourselves become healed, revived, restored.

A legend of the Far East tells of a sorrowing woman who came to a wise man with a heartrending plea that he return to her her only son, whom she had just lost. He told her that he could comply with her request on one condition. She would have to bring him a mustard seed taken from a home entirely free from sorrow. The woman set out on her quest. Years elapsed and she did not return. One day, the wise man chanced upon her, but he hardly recognized her, for now she looked so serene, so radiant. He greeted her and asked her why she never kept their appointment. "This is what happened," she said to the sage. "In search of the mustard seed, I came into homes so burdened with sorrow and trouble that I just could not walk out. Who, better than I, could understand how heavy was the burden they bore? Who, better than I, could offer them the sympathy they needed? So I stayed on in each home as long as I could be of service. And," she added apologetically, "please do not be angry, but I never again thought about our appointment."

The world is not fair to Israel. Every nation wages a war to win. And when it wins, it conquers, and when it conquers, it occupies, and when it occupies, it secures territory necessary for its defense. Every country, but Israel may not. Saul Bellow once said, "It is only the Jew who is expected to be exceptionally exceptional." We need to make the world more fair to Israel and to the Jewish people.

Life is unfair to families who are not together at this holy season because of singleness, divorce, death, and alienation.

Life is unfair to children who are not impressive achievers. We see our own ego rewarded by the brilliance of our children. If they fall below our expectations, they feel unloved and rejected.

Life is unfair to slow learners and those with learning disabilities.

Life is unfair to many older people, particularly those who are infirm and weak and who suffer from neglect and emptiness.

Life is unfair to the disenchanted and disaffected young, who have yet to find their way in the world.

Life is unfair to those whose lives are ravaged with the suffering of terminal illness—and to their loved ones.

Life is unfair to those whose careers and work are threatened by unemployment, inflation, and recession.

Life is unfair to the afflicted and the handicapped. And who is not afflicted, and who is not handicapped?

Life is unfair to the thousands of families who lost a loved one in the tragedy of September 11. We grieve for them. We offer our prayer that the Almighty grant them healing and solace.

For all these and more, we should make the world more fair, more sensitive, more compassionate.

Shall we respond in bitterness or in rebellion? Shall we respond with submission and acquiescence? Shall we avert our gaze? I read a story of a young man sitting in a crowded subway with his hands covering his face. A little old lady standing nearby said to him, "Young man, are you ill?" To which the young man replied, "No. It's just that it hurts me to see an old lady standing." Of course he had an alternative to avoid seeing an old lady stand. He could have arisen and given her his seat. He could have made her world and his a little more fair.

Marcel Proust wrote, "In my cowardice I became at once a man, and I did what all grown men do when we are face-to-face with suffering and injustice. I preferred not to see them." We often yield to the temptation to ignore life's unfairness, to avert our gaze.

I have a friend whom I admire as a resolute, positive person. Not tough, but strong; not given to philosophy, but thoughtful and wise. He said something to me once that left an enduring impact on me: "When a friend of mine is unhappy, I want to know why"—because that concern makes life less unfair.

As we make the world more fair, we discover that we belong together. The weak need the strong; the sick, the well; the ignorant, the learned; the frightened, the brave. The only way to make life more fair is to affirm that it is a common gift in which all of us must share.

So often, life deals such crushing blows, and our immediate outcry is, "Why me? Why now? How can a merciful God permit this to happen?" These are the wrong questions. The real question is, What do I do with what I have left? A person who has the courage to answer this question can respond to crushing blows with a determined response.

There is a story of a man who looked up at the heavens and said, "Dear God, there is so much pain and anguish in Your world—why don't you send help?" And God answered, "I did send help—I sent you." What can we do to make the world more fair? What can we do to enlarge the boundaries of what is good, right, and decent?

For the world should be made more fair. And if God will not do it, then we will undertake to do it for Him and on His behalf.

Our tradition teaches us that when God created the world, He left it unfinished. God left us an incomplete world. But as we attempt to improve it, we come to see with ever greater clarity that injustice is not basic to the scheme of things but a stage in the world's development for man to transcend. We begin to understand that God, too, is fighting injustice with us, through us.

Dr. Paul Scherer describes a train wreck. One of the passengers was a famous surgeon who escaped unhurt. We see him standing before a seriously injured fellow passenger. Helplessly watching the hurt man slowly die, the surgeon exclaimed time and again—"My God, if I just had my instruments." So God looks at our world and says, "All this can be changed if only I had my instruments." We are His instruments, His tools, His resources. This is both our burden and our glory.

And those were the words that concluded our farewell to Debbie— the words of the Kaddish "B'alma Di V'ra Chirutay" in the world which He created by His will. May His Kingdom of truth and justice, of compassion and peace, come speedily in our time.

In the end, we realize that God and we are not opponents—He, the injurer, we the injured. No, we are partners in a continuing enterprise, in Tikkun Olam, in improving the world, in achieving a society in which injustice will be no more and the world will be fair. In this great effort, we arrive at the noblest discovery possible to us as human beings. We, the creatures of the master of the universe, are yet co-workers in a glorious adventure with Him in the building of His kingdom on earth.

Conquering Our Fears

What brings us to the synagogue on these High Holidays? There are many reasons: expression of solidarity with the Jewish people, a sense of loyalty to our heritage, an affirmation of faith in the ideals of our tradition. But there is one theme or motif which resonates in the words and melodies of our liturgy with the most powerful and universal of emotions.

These holy days are called "Yomin Noraim," Days of Awe. Those who enter the synagogue in worship are stirred by feelings of reverence and fear elicited by the contemplation of the future, of the uncertainties and contingencies of life. The service reaches its climax as we recite the passage from "une tanah tokef": "On the first day of the year it is inscribed, and on the day of atonement, it is sealed. How many shall pass away, and how many shall be born. Who shall live and who shall die. Who shall be tranquil, and who shall be harassed. Who shall be at ease, and who shall be afflicted. Who shall become poor, and who shall become rich. Who shall be brought low, and who shall be raised up."

Even the angels tremble with terror on these days of judgment. We mark the New Year not with revelry and mindless frivolity, as is a custom for the secular New Year. But we face the possibilities of loss and pain, suffering and sorrow.

What is our state of mind as we reflect upon the year that has ended and the year that now begins? I sense a troubling anxiety which darkens the edges of our perceptions, which casts long shadows over the landscape of our existence. We have witnessed many threats to our tranquility in a world that is subject to unknowable and unforeseeable political, social, and economic forces.

The terrorist attack on a Pan American airplane in Karachi, followed by a wave of bombings in Paris, causes us deep concern. Worshipers in the synagogue in Istanbul were murdered on a Sabbath morning in September. We are outraged and saddened and angered that no place, not even a house of God, is safe anymore.

In this nuclear age, we are concerned about human survival and the proliferation of atomic weapons. But after the technological accident at Chernobyl, we wonder about the effects of the radioactive material that has leaked into the atmosphere. We wonder about nuclear accidents.

As Jews, we have much to fear, too, for our group survival is constantly challenged. Anti-Semitism here and abroad has not disappeared. The fate of Soviet Jews hangs in the balance. Our brothers and sisters, prisoners of conscience, are literally held hostage by a repressive Soviet regime. American Jewry faces internal dangers that are no less serious: by intermarriage, low birthrate, Jewish illiteracy, and apathy to Jewish values.

But I do not propose to speak about our collective fears. Rather, I want to address myself to some of the personal fears that afflict us, that paralyze us, that diminish us.

But first, I share a song which was very popular in Israel after the Yom Kippur War. The words are these: "The whole world is just one narrow bridge, and the main thing is not to be afraid."

The song has a strange history. The words were originally written by Rabbi Nachman of Bratislava, who lived in the Ukraine, the area in which Chernobyl is located, more than a century and a half ago.

It's a very tight walk, this journey through life. We do it only once, without precedent or experience, and it's full of danger. You can make it if you don't panic.

There are so many dangers, so many risks, that all of us have moments of fear. I remember an interview several years ago that Dr. DeBakey gave after one of his first heart transplants. The reporters asked him, "How is the patient doing?" And he said, "He is resting comfortably." They asked him, "How much longer do you expect him to be on the critical list?" And he answered very simply, "He'll be on the critical list for as long as he lives."

I felt that Dr. DeBakey was not only talking about a patient, he was talking about all of us. We are all on the critical list for as long as we live. Your son and daughter take the car, and they come back ten minutes late, and you die a thousand deaths until you see that they are all right. Young people wonder how old they have to be before their parents stop saying, "Be careful," when they leave the house. Parents apparently sleep better when you tell them when you will be home so they can schedule their fears. They know exactly what time to start worrying.

The fear of death. The holiday prayers remind us dramatically of our mortality. Several years ago, in a popular film called *Four Seasons*, there was a character, a fun-loving dentist, who seems to be a buffoon without a serious side to him. In a moment of revelation and earnestness, however, he reveals his deep-seated fears of illness and death. The audience realizes that his frivolous exterior is a facade that masks his intense terror of dying, and the audience identifies with him very strongly.

Paradoxically, we have more fears about our own well-being despite the great advances in health and medicine. Our grandparents were worried about three or four serious illnesses. We live in an environment teaming with microbes, pollen, bacteria, air pollution, acid rain, and a multitude of diseases that no one knew existed forty years ago.

We are committed to a profession or a business or a career, and we try to cope with the fear of failure. We have accepted criteria of success. We see our friends of yesterday rising, and we fear that we will be left behind. We are terrified of failure.

The midlife crisis is another fear that is pervasive these days, especially as longevity has become an American blessing. But this is a mixed blessing. I see men and women who suffer from the fear of growing old, of losing youthful power and zest, who are terrified that life is passing them by. In response to that fear, they break up marriages and families. They abandon relationships; they reject the traditional values that offer stability and meaning to life.

We used to think of childhood as a carefree and happy period in human development. This is simply not so. Today's young people live with anxiety and fear and stress that are unique to our age. They must cope with pressures and temptations for engaging in the use of forbidden drugs, promiscuity, and defiance of moral standards. Many suffer from a lack of self-esteem, feelings of unworthiness and inadequacy. In the spring of this year, I spoke with the young people in the religious school about teenage suicides, which have risen dramatically in recent years. I was simultaneously enlightened, shocked, and saddened by what I learned in this frank and open encounter.

After all this, I am reminded of a cartoon I once saw in which a newscaster began his evening report with the words "As a public service, we are not reporting the news tonight."

Rabbi Nachman is right. The whole world is just one narrow bridge, and the main thing is not to be afraid.

How can you not be afraid when you live in such a dangerous world? Some people, when they realize that the world is just such a narrow span, freeze and can't go forward; others try to turn around and go back; some jump off to their own destruction. But Rabbi Nachman says you should know the world is a narrow bridge. And yet, you should move forward and not be afraid until you get to the other side.

That's easier said than done. How do you overcome fear? When life is so dangerous, how do you not panic? To that question, our answer is one word. The same answer that Moses and David and Jeremiah and Akiva and all the other generations of the faithful would have given. How can you live in such a dangerous world? The answer is "Bitachon," which means trust. How can you live in such a dangerous world? The answer is, God.

There are a lot of different definitions of God and religion. But the shortest and simplest definition of God that I know is this: "God is the

One who enables us to live without fears. God is that miraculous power that enables us to believe that even if today is terrifying, tomorrow will be better."

What is the world's most beloved psalm? The Lord is my shepherd. What is the most celebrated line? "Yea, though I walk through the valley of the shadow of death, even then, I shall not fear, for thou art with me." God does not redeem us from death. We will all die one day. But He redeems us from the shadow of death, from letting our lives be paralyzed by the fear of death.

A philosopher, Horace Kallen, marked his seventy-third birthday by writing, "There are persons who shape their lives by the fear of death. There are persons who shape their lives by the joy and satisfaction of life. The former live dying; the latter die living. I know that fate may stop me tomorrow, but death is an irrelevant contingency. Whenever it comes, I intend to die living."

Whatever else religion is, and it is many things—a moral code, a set of observances, a way of understanding the universe, the witness of a people to moral idealism—whatever else religion is, and it is all of these things, at its very center is the message "Al-Tira." Do not fear. Religion is the answer and the antidote to fear. What it says very simply is that whatever may happen to you, you are not alone. Wherever you go, you cannot go beyond God, and whatever you do, you need not fear.

If there is one word that summarizes the history of the Jewish people, and its most inspiring achievement, even to those unfamiliar with its beliefs, the word is *courage*. There is a story of three men who were on the shores of the Mediterranean when the shocking news came that as a result of some radical shift in the earth's composition, the Mediterranean Sea was about to overflow and destroy all life. The Spaniard went to his house of worship to offer a final prayer. The Italian decided that a glass of wine would be in order. The Jew said, "I will have to learn how to live under water."

Courage is embodied by Anatole Scharansky, who is free today primarily because of his own inner strength. He defied the Soviet authorities, he was punished with cruel and unusual punishment, and even when threatened with death, he never betrayed his soul.

But courage is more than such dramatic heroic acts. Courage is the willingness to overcome fear and to risk failure and create a new and better reality. The Bible describes how spies came back from the land of Canaan and said, "We shall not prevail; we shall be defeated; we shall be overcome." Of course, there was a risk of failure, and courage means our ability to accept that risk in the belief that, ultimately, we or the generations of the future will triumph.

Thus, real courage is the ability to pick ourselves up after failure and loss and to go on about the business of living.

Courage is the woman who goes on with her life even after her husband walks out the door. Courage is the businessman who rises up from bankruptcy to plan new plans and to begin new ventures. Courage is the mourner who loses a dear one but who hasn't lost his love for life.

Courage is found in unexpected places and wears many faces.

"Sometimes," says one of Sholom Aleichem's characters, "You have to go on living even if it kills you."

Sometimes courage is dressed up as stubborn loyalty during weeks, months, and years of ministering to a sick child or to a helpless parent.

Of one thing we can be sure. No life will go very far before it needs courage. No life will reach very high without it.

Life is all risk. The act of living is truly a risky business. And all of us would like to resist risk taking.

The story was told of the mother who couldn't get her son to go to school. "Why won't you go?" He said, "It's too risky; the children call me names—they make signs and gestures behind my back. Give me three good reasons why I should go." "Look," said the mother. "First, I won't take no for an answer. Second, you are forty-four years old, and third, you are the principal." Risk taking is the essential first step in making decisions, crossing new frontiers of knowledge, accepting responsibility, discovering who we are and what we can do. If we spent half as much time learning how to take risks as we spent avoiding them, we wouldn't have nearly so much to fear in life. You don't have to wait for emergencies or momentous occasions to learn the art of risk taking. You can practice it daily by standing up for what you believe, by making firm decisions instead of procrastinating, by doing something you always wanted to do and never dared. To venture is to risk anxiety, but not to venture is to lose yourself.

But sometimes we risk and we lose. In a shattering moment everything can change. It's at that moment that I have seen real courage.

When we enter the synagogue, we can hear the voices of all the generations who have preceded us. In their worst moment of doubt, they found strength by their deep and abiding faith in God. "Fear not, my servant, Jacob" are the words that they carried in their hearts. They believed in God and surmounted their most terrifying fears—in Roman days, in medieval ghettos, in crusades and expulsions, in inquisitions, and in Warsaw's flaming ghetto. When they sang, "Ani Ma-Amin"— "I Believe," they transcended the most desperate of their fears. If they had not had such faith, where would the Jewish people be today? If we feared anyone, it was our God. "Uv'Chen Ten Pah-Decha." But by fearing Him, we learn to shed our dread of human oppressors and tyrants.

Life is an adventure, and often it is a fearful adventure with many perils. But the enemy is not danger. It is fear. The whole world is one narrow bridge, but the main thing is not to be afraid. So help us, God, stay with us till we get to the other side. We will find in you the power who will not let us succumb to despair. We will find in you the voice which urges us to hold on, to keep going. When we are bewildered, we will find in you our hope for guidance. When we are bewildered, we will find in you our hope for healing. When we are bereaved, we will find in you our hope for solace. When we are confronted with the inescapable fact of our weakness and mortality, we shall find in you our hope for strength and eternity.

As we face the awesome uncertainties of the New Year, we do not know what the future holds, but we do know who holds the future. He whom we can depend on to grant us sufficient courage, sufficient wisdom, sufficient strength to confront that future heroically and to live it bravely. We can move forward across the narrow bridge with the faith of the psalmist: "The Lord is my light and my help. Whom shall I fear? The Lord is the stronghold of my life, of whom shall I be afraid?"

Taking Control of Your Life

Each year, at this time, I sense the powerful stream of loyalty and faith that flows from the hearts of all and fills the synagogue with sanctity, reverence, and joy.

Boarding a train, a young man sits down beside a dignified-looking gentleman. "Can you tell me the time?" the young man asked.

His companion looks him up and down and exclaims, "No, I forbid it." "Forbid what?" the young man asks in perplexity. The older one sighs and says, "All right, I'll explain. If I tell you the time, you will start to talk about the weather. After that, politics, and soon, we will discover that we both are Jews. So then, what happens? Naturally, I invite you to my home where you meet my beautiful, irresistible daughter. Of course, you fall in love, and finally, you ask me for her hand in marriage. Well, I'm telling you here and now, I forbid it! I absolutely refuse to let my daughter marry a man who can't even afford a watch!"

We all know what day this is, what hour this is. This is the time for Chesbon Ha-Nefesh, for spiritual reckoning.

The "une tanah tokef" prayer written about eight hundred years ago sets forth the great themes of this season. With its haunting refrain, it conveys the image of a courtroom where we stand before the Supreme Judge of the Universe. He opens the book of remembrance, and the record speaks for itself. He reviews the story of every living being and determines the destiny of every creature.

"On Rosh Hashanah, it is written and on Yom Kippur it is sealed—how many shall leave this world, how many shall enter it; who shall rise and who shall fall; who shall be at ease and who afflicted; who shall be humbled, who exalted."

This is Yom Ha-Din, Judgment Day. God, the Judge, is ever present, although not visible, and His authority is proclaimed with awe and reverence.

But this is an unusual courtroom. We are not commanded to be silent; we are not restricted in our response. We are encouraged to talk, argue, explain, beseech, and entreat the Ruler of the Universe. We are stimulated to do everything in our power to persuade the Heavenly Judge to view us with His favor and to change His decision—so to speak even after the severe decree has been pronounced.

We don't accept the bitterness of the unfavorable verdict. We challenge the Judge, we plead our case, we ask for blessing and fulfillment. Indeed, the intent of the prayer is not to express resignation to our harsh fate. The opposite is true. The message of this day is to take personal control of our lives. The conclusion of the prayer is a call to action.

There are three ways in which the evil decree is overcome. *Teshubah,* or repentance, which means to take personal responsibility for our conduct and return to the highest level of which we are capable.

Tefillah, or prayer, which means to restore our relationship with God and return to Him in faith and trust.

Tzedakah, or charity, which means to restore our relationship with our fellow man and respond with loving-kindness to need, want, and deprivation and advance the welfare of the community.

How do we take control of our lives? First we must recognize our own potential. Dr. Abraham Maslow, noted psychologist, estimated that the average human being achieves only 7 percent of his potential. Should we rest content with such a meager harvest?

Rebbe Shlomo of Karlin, one of the great Hasidic masters, once startled his disciples by asking them an unusual question: "What is the most grievous sin a Jew can commit?"

His disciples reflected for a while, and then they presented their respective, predictable answers: "Murder," said one. "Idolatry," said the second. "Desecrating the name of the Almighty," suggested the third.

The rabbi shook his head after each answer, and when finally all the disciples had been heard, the rabbi gave his own answer.

"The most grievous sin a Jew can commit is to forget the biblical verse 'You are children of the Lord, your God.'"

What is the point of this story? To look upon ourselves as children of God is to invest our lives with their fullest potentiality. In a word, we achieve as we believe. A person's outlook is determined by his attitude. We can either make ourselves miserable or make ourselves strong.

Our severest handicap is a distorted self-image. When we think of ourselves as incapable, unlovable, unsuccessful, we tend to become all these things. However, when we have a positive sense of self, our achievements will reflect that self-appraisal. We tend to become what we imagine ourselves to be.

But, if you want to take control of your life, you must believe that you are a child of God.

The Siddur echoes this philosophy, which finds expression in one of the preliminary morning blessings: "Praised are you, Lord our God, Ruler of the Universe, who fashioned me in your image. "What a magnificent statement. To begin each morning with this declaration is to be reminded of our unique, intimate, and personal relationship with our Creator. We are reminded of our unlimited potentiality, our sacred responsibility, our inherent dignity.

This theme is articulated by the Torah reading of today, which begins with an affirmation of life under the most impossible conditions. "And the Lord remembered Sara as He had promised, and she did conceive and bear a child."

That birth was promised by God under circumstances which made the promise seem absurd, ridiculous. God informed Abraham when he was ninety-nine and when Sara was eighty-nine, "Next year, when you will be one hundred and Sara will be ninety, you are going to have a surprise—it will be a blessing—you will have a son. Sara is going to give birth to a baby." The Bible tells us that when Sara heard this, *Vatizchak*, she giggled, she laughed. Sara might well have said, "I can't have a child. My 'biological clock' stopped ticking forty years ago. Don't tell me that rubbish; it's impossible; I can't."

It must have been obvious that Abraham felt the same way. He may have already been walking with a cane. He was suffering from lower back pain. His arthritis was a constant nuisance. Talk of him fathering a baby sounded ridiculous to him. But God has his plans.

Bob Talbert's column recently noted a man in Grand Rapids reading from the Bible, the Book of Genesis, to his five-year-old granddaughter. When he finished, she appeared lost in thought. So he asked, "What do you think of it?" She looked up and replied, "I love it. You never know what God is going to do next, do you?"

The Bible says that God told Abraham, "Hayipalay May—Ha Shem Davar?"—"Is anything too hard for God? Abraham, never say to me the word 'Can't.' It is the most vulgar four-letter word in the dictionary. Learn to erase the last letter, the letter 't,' and you'll learn that 'can't' becomes 'can'—the impossible becomes the possible, the unfeasible becomes the feasible, and the unachievable becomes the achievable. Your attitude is the most important thing."

I recall a poem I heard as a boy.

> If you think you are beaten, you are;
> If you think you dare not, you don't.
> If you'd like to win but think you can't,
> It's almost a cinch you won't.
> If you think you'll lose, you're lost;
> For out in the world we find success begins with a fellow's will;
> It's all in the state of mind.

I share a colleague's distinction of the difference between wishing someone Mazel or a Brachah. In the former, either you have Mazel or you don't, and no amount of wishing, complaining, or begging can change that. As for the latter, Brachah, you can create your own blessing and work at it and be your own blessing. You can take charge of your own life.

I recognize that we do not all have the same opportunities. Some of us live with disabilities, many of us with burdens, all of us with limitations, but consider this—life can be understood as a game of cards. We have no control over the hand dealt us. We do, however, have control over how we play the hand. There is no point in blaming the dealer for a bad hand. The trick is to play it out with all the skill and determination of our command. This is what it means to "take responsibility."

Golda Meir once said, "I was never a beauty. There was a time when I was sorry about that, when I was old enough to understand the importance of it. And looking in my mirror, I realized it was something I was never going to have. Then I found what I wanted to do in life, and being pretty no longer had any importance. It was much later that I realized that not being beautiful was a blessing in disguise. It forced me to develop my inner resources. I came to understand that women who cannot lean on their beauty and need to make something of themselves on their own have the advantage." She compensated by cultivating the spiritual qualities that she possessed in such amazing abundance.

This summer, a twenty-nine-year-old paraplegic, paralyzed from the waist down since a 1982 climbing accident, finished a grueling eight-day climb up El Capitan, one of the high mountains in Yosemite National Park.

Mark Wellman became the first paraplegic to make the thirty-two-hundred-foot climb, doing seven thousand pull-ups on ropes placed by his partner.

Wellman told reporters, "You have a dream, and you know the only way that dream is going to happen is if you just do it . . . even if it is six inches at a time."

To take control over our lives, we need to begin with the ability to dream dreams and to use our imagination. The message of our prophets so often begins with the word *chazon*, a vision. The prophet offers us a vision of what life could be. It's not an illusion or a fantasy. It is rather a projection into the future of what could be achieved if we would summon forth our will and determination. This kind of imagination is within the reach of each of us. In fact, it is part of the Jewish heritage. We are, after all, the people of Jacob, who envisioned a ladder stretching from the earth to the heavens. We are descendants of the people of the prophets, who foretold a day "when the lion would lie down with the lamb, when nation would no longer lift up sword against nation, neither would they learn war anymore." George Bernard Shaw wrote, "Some look at the world as it is and ask why? I dream of a world that can be and ask, why not?"

The second step on the road to self-mastery is courage.

For most of us, this word conjures images of soldiers going over the top, or other feats of daring, but courage is much more than this. It is the willingness to risk failure or disapproval in the effort to create a new and better reality. Robert Louis Stevenson said it well: "You cannot run away from a weakness; you must sometimes fight it out or perish. And if that be so, why not know where you stand?"

That is real courage, the ability to pick ourselves up after failure and loss and to go on about the business of living.

Can we ever be certain of success? The young man who was buying an engagement ring asked that it be engraved "From Henry to Clara." "Take my advice," said the jeweler, "and just have 'From Henry'." A worthy life takes courage.

This kind of courage is within the reach of every one of us Look around you, and you will find courage everywhere. I see it in any one of us who feels the burden of past mistakes and failures and yet resolves to be better, stronger, and wiser in the year to come. I see it in that remarkable human resilience which enables us to withstand pain, to suffer loss, to confront death itself, and still go on singing and sharing and celebrating life.

A life without courage and risk is a life over which we exercise no control. Consider this whimsical statement.

> There was a very cautious man
> Who never laughed or played.
> He never risked, he never tried,
> He never sang or prayed.
> And when he one day passed away,
> His insurance was denied.
> For since he never really lived,
> They claimed he never died.

But imagination and courage are not enough. If we are to achieve control over our lives, a third quality is necessary—discipline—a word we don't hear much about today. By this, I don't mean the enforced discipline of parent or teacher or institution, the controlling and modifying of our behavior by threats and promises. I mean self-discipline—the strength of purpose which keeps us at the task even though it is always easier to give it up. Many of us tend to jump from one thing to the next, staying with it only so long as it continues to amuse us, abandoning it the moment it ceases to be diverting or begins to make demands on us. Personal growth requires a sense of discipline, commitment to stay with the task until it is done and done well.

One of Adlai Stevenson's favorite stories concerned a man who was being interviewed on his hundredth birthday. Naturally he was asked to what he attributed his longevity. He answered, "I have never smoked, consumed alcohol, or overeaten. I go to bed early and I get up early."

"You know," said the reporter, "I had an uncle who lived exactly that way, and he only lived to the age of seventy. To what do you attribute that?"

The old man replied, "He just didn't keep it up long enough."

This is the wisdom of the Jewish people—that nothing of consequence will ever come to us without discipline and perseverance. We believe in mitzvoth, in commandments which provide the pattern to follow as we weave the fabric of our lives. These give us strength and power and bless our lives with meaning.

I ask each person in the name of our tradition to remember that since we are all children of God, we should take the "can't" out of our spiritual vocabulary. Each of us is asked to climb one more step, to move up one more rung on the ladder of holiness.

What can we offer? I ask for simple things—not radical changes. One more Mitzvah, and then another. We can take our choice: a word of blessing, a prayer, an hour of study, a Sabbath service, a festival celebration, a chapter of the Bible, a verse of Scripture, the skill of reading Hebrew, a deed of loving kindness, a visit to the sick, a word of encouragement, an outstretched hand.

I invite parents to appreciate and experience the heritage of Judaism which they seek to transmit to their children. I turn to the unmarried, and to the single parent, and to the senior citizens, and to Jews by choice, and to teenagers, and to college students, and to both the older and younger generations to increase their Jewish awareness, experience, and joy in some tangible form in the course of this year. And when this happens, we will emerge as a challenging and inspiring model of what Jewish life could become in this land. The secret of success is in the words of Dr. Abraham Joshua Heschel: "Do as much as you can, and then do a little more than you can."

> The Judge is waiting.
> The time is now.
> The reward is great.

The verdict is in our hands.
May we be worthy of a life of blessing.

Promises

Somewhere today a woman is saying, "I would like to dump this marriage and start over with somebody who knows how to love me. God knows this guy I've been married to has not given me the love I need, the love I deserve." And she wonders about the promise made years ago standing under the huppah. What does it mean these days—to make a promise?

Somewhere today a father is saying to himself, "I want my impossible son to get out of the house and never come back. God knows I have tried to be patient and understanding, but he is driving me out of my mind!" And he thinks back to the promise he made when he held that newborn baby in his arms—the promise to care for and nurture him, the promise to provide for him whatever he might need. What does it mean these days to make a promise?

Maybe somewhere today people still keep their promises. Maybe somewhere today there are people who still choose not to quit when the going gets tough because they promised once to see it through. Yes, maybe somewhere there are people who still dare to make promises and care enough about the promises they make. Maybe. What does it mean these days to make a promise?

I wish to speak about promises. Ironic? Last night began with Kol Nidre, Judaism's most famous prayer for the nullification of promises.

Today, I choose to speak about keeping our promises? No, it really is not so strange at all—Kol Nidre proves how seriously we Jews take our promises. Kol Nidre is the heartfelt cry to God written by Jews in a time of duress when they were forced under pain of death to make promises to convert, promises that were made with their lips but never felt in their hearts. Yet because these Jews took the act of promising so seriously, they felt the pain of not keeping their promises, even made under conditions like this. No, we Jews have always taken our promises very seriously, and this Yom Kippur day is the perfect time to consider how far we have strayed.

"What a marvelous thing a promise is!" says pastor and professor Lewis B. Smedes: "When a person makes a promise, he reaches out into an unpredictable future and makes one thing predictable: he will be there even when being there costs him more than he wants to pay. When a person makes a promise, he stretches himself out into circumstances that no one can control and controls at least one thing: he will be there no matter what the circumstances turn out to be. With one single word of promise, a person creates an island of certainty in a sea of uncertainty."

When you make a promise, you take a hand in creating your own future. When I make a promise, I am acting on the assumption that my future is not predetermined; that I am not totally bound to the fateful combination of x's and y's in my genetic code. When I make a promise, I refuse to surrender my relationships with people I love to the wayward drives of my subconscious. When I make a promise, I act in freedom. I create a future of my own and an identity of my own. I create my identity as this woman's husband and that child's father and that man's friend. Our culture tries to tell us we can be real selves only if we claim our right to self-satisfaction and self-fulfillment. But a free self knows that he becomes a genuine self by making commitments to other people—promises that he intends to keep even when keeping them exacts a price.

The story is told of the young man who is brought into the family business and shows up the first day to be given "the lecture" by his father. "Son," the father begins, "this business was started by your grandfather and maintained with blood, sweat, and tears by your uncles and myself. And as you now take your place in it, it is important that you learn the two words upon which this business has been built—integrity and wisdom!" To which the son inquires, "So what is the difference?" "Integrity," explains the father, "means that your word is your bond. If you make a promise, you keep it, even if keeping that promise means costing the business time and sacrifice and effort. Son, integrity means that we keep the promises that we make!" "So, what is wisdom?" "Son," says the father, "wisdom means knowing never ever under any circumstances to make such a promise!"

But the truth is that a promise that costs nothing is no promise—and we are known by the promises we keep. Some people ask, "Who am I?" and expect an answer to come from their feelings. Some people ask, "Who am I?" and expect the answer to come from their accomplishments. Other people ask, "Who am I?" and expect the answer to come from what other people think about them. A person who dares to make and keep promises discovers who he is by the promises he has made and kept to other people.

What you desire is not what you are. Desires rise and fall and change so fast that they can only tell you what you want at any trembling moment, but knowing what you want is not the same as knowing what you are.

It is the power of promise making that creates a lasting and genuine identity for us.

In *A Man for All Seasons*, that brilliant play about Sir Thomas More, More's daughter, Meg, begged him to save his skin by going back on a promise that he made. His answer tells us how dangerous it is to make light of a promise, no matter how risky it is to keep it: "Ah, Meg, when a man takes an oath, he holds his own self in his hands, like water, and when he opens his hands he need not hope to find himself again."

We are our promises, and we lose hold of ourselves when we take no pains to keep them.

"The person who makes a vow," said Chesterton, "makes an appointment with himself at some distant time and place and he gives up his freedom in order to keep that appointment." You freely tie yourself down so that other persons can be free to trust that you will keep your promise to them.

On this sort of trust, the whole human family depends. The future of the human race hangs on a promise. Is there a happy ending to the human romance? It depends completely on a word spoken, a promise made.

Only one thing can assure us that the story of mankind will not end in global disaster. One thing gives us hope that one day the world will finally work right for everyone and that the human family will discover peace and love and justice and freedom together. That one thing is a promise made and a promise kept. But I fear that we are still some distance from that day.

It all began some four thousand years ago, halfway around the world, when a lonely single individual named Avraham made a promise. In one single shining moment, the direction of world history was changed by this one man who burned his bridges to his past and gambled his destiny, and that of future generations as well, on the reliability of a promise he heard from a stranger in the wilderness. A voice that said, "Lech Lecha"—"Go forward and trust in Me!"

It was some thirty-two hundred years ago when this was reaffirmed by another individual, alone, frightened, running for his life, Moshe, who was stopped in his tracks by a bush in the wilderness that did not want to stop burning. Moshe was brought to attention by the voice of an invisible, ineffable Someone calling him to return to Egypt and lead his too long neglected people out of slavery. "Go forward and trust in Me!" said the voice.

Moshe was understandably skeptical. "What is your name?" he asked the stranger. "The people whom you ask me to lead will need some identification." And the name came from behind the flame; it came in a word of four cryptic Hebrew consonants that have defied translation— "Alef hey yud hey," "Eheye asher eheye"—"I am who I am," the scholars have rendered it. But Moshe was not a philosopher. He was a

Hebrew shepherd who knew that everything depended on whether this stranger God who was sending him to lead a slave nation to freedom; who was sending him to confront the most powerful man on earth, the great pharaoh of Egypt, and to demand of him to "Let my people go!"—Moshe knew that everything depended on whether this God, who could not be seen and rarely heard, could be trusted.

"Go forward and trust in Me!" said God. But that is not all He said. At this most critical juncture in human history, God wanted to tell Moshe that He was a God who made promises and kept the promises He made. So the most likely translation of His name goes something like this: "Eheye asher eheye"—"I am the One who will be there with you." This is God's identity; this is who and what God is: a promise maker and a promise keeper.

For the past thirty-two hundred years, this has been what has kept us going, what has maintained us through long and dark nights of oppression and hatred. This is what has sustained us through exile and persecution, through pogrom and Holocaust, and brought us to return and resurrection. The one thing that has kept us as a people is our belief in the promise of the stranger in the wilderness, the "One who will be there with you"—the One who has been there with us.

When a child is born to us, we bring him on the eighth day for a Brith Milah, and for a girl, we bring her in the presence of the Torah itself. We hold up that child—that precious gift of life upon which our entire future depends—and we proclaim, "Kshem shenichnas l'brit keyn yikanes l'torah, l'chupah u'lemassim tovim"—"Just as this child has been privileged to be brought into the Covenant of good deeds today— so may he/she yet attain the privilege of a life of Torah, of marriage, and of a life of goodness." When a child is born we bring them to the synagogue, and a promise is made. A promise that we promise to keep.

And when a child reaches the age of adulthood, a Bar Mitzvah, a Bat Mitzvah, is celebrated. The first time we brought them to the bimah in our arms, but this time they walk on their own. The first time we spoke for them; this time they speak for themselves—and they affirm with their own mouths the promise of the ages. And on their wedding day we bring them back to the Bimah with their loved one, "bchirat libo"—their heart's choice, their life's mate. We bring them back to the sanctuary to remind them what a promise really means.

We say to them, "Dearest, precious child. Remember what this place stands for. This is a place of promises. When you were born we, your parents, brought you here and promised to raise you as a Jew, to help you become a mentsch. When you celebrated your Bar or Bat Mitzvah, you affirmed that promise yourself. And now you come with the love of your life, and this place proclaims the seriousness of the promise you are about to make. Marriage is not a game. And we cannot promise that it will be easy. Marriage is a serious and lifelong undertaking that is often entered into too lightly and, nowadays, too often ended when troubles begin to mount. Sometimes, to be sure, marriages must end; sometimes marriages should end. Sometimes, we can make no other choice. But when another choice can be made, we should make it. Because, precious child, keeping our promises matters. Because, precious child, our husbands and our wives matter. And because, of course, the children matter."

Now I know I must step lightly in the next few moments. I am navigating dangerous waters if I choose to say more on the subject of marriage and commitment. The story is told of the itinerant preacher who gave a sermon on Sunday morning to a group of chicken farmers on the eighth commandment—"Thou shalt not steal." The sermon was so outstanding, the preacher was so dynamic, that they invited him back the following week to give the same sermon so others could hear it. He returned and delivered the same sermon, changing only one word—he titled it: "Thou Shalt Not Steal Chickens!"—and they hated it; those chicken farmers couldn't understand why they had liked it so much the week before. When sermons get too close to home, they can become a little unpleasant—and to speak on marriage and divorce is indeed dangerous territory, so I shall choose my words carefully.

It is certainly not that we take our marriages lightly. The majority of Americans will be married for some part of their lives. (Some 78 percent of American family households are the households of married people, and I suspect that number is even higher in our community.) And even though the divorce rate has lately been about half of the marriage rate, still, nine out of ten married people tell pollsters they would marry the same people again. Marriage is still an institution of enormous beauty, even if that beauty is too often marred by human fallibility. Why, after all, do we cry at weddings? Is it not because we can scarcely bear the beauty of the union that we are witnessing—and also because hard experience has taught us of its fragility? We marry, says Yale law professor Stephen Carter, "out of hope, or fear, or desire, or desperation, and certainly out of love; and yet I believe that in every marriage, no matter how begun, there is that kernel of possibility that this is the one for the ages." I meet and counsel every couple I marry prior to the huppah, and not once have I ever spoken to a couple that has intended their marriage to be anything less than forever.

So how do we explain divorces? Do you know the story about the man down in Miami who says to his friend, "How is your daughter, the one who is married to a CPA?" The man says, "Oh, she divorced him." The friend says, "Oh, I'm sorry." The man says, "Oh, but she married a lawyer." The friend says, "Mazel Tov." The man says, "Thank you, but then she divorced him." The friend says, "I'm sorry." The man says, "Thank you, but then she married a doctor." The friend says, "A CPA? A doctor? A lawyer? Fun ein kint, azoilfil nachas!" For the benefit of the Yiddishly challenged: "From one child, so much *nachas!*—so much joy." But the truth is that it is not such *nachas,* especially if it is your daughter or son, and it is not at all funny if it is you. So many broken hearts, so many broken homes, so many broken promises.

Many can be explained by the simple fact that we humans are not perfect. We make mistakes. As Jews, we recognize this fact, and there is a mechanism for divorce in our sacred tradition because we recognize that sometimes, with even the most honorable of intentions, we need to start anew; there is just no hope for reconciliation and rehabilitation. I pass no judgment on anyone today. But as much as I know that many, maybe even most, of the divorces today are unavoidable, I know that some of them were, and that pains me greatly.

A promise is an indication of a determination to try. Sometimes for all our effort and all our good intentions we will fail, but I do not understand those who make so little effort to try.

A man was once informing me of his intention to divorce his wife. And when I pressed him as to whether everything possible had been done to save the marriage and to maintain the promise, he said, "Rabbi, after all, promises are made to be broken." Any man who thinks that promises were made to be broken should see what it does to his family. Any woman who thinks that it is not worth the emotional effort to even try to save the marriage should see the pain and hurt and loss that are the result of every divorce. And there are more than a few people who will gladly testify to the truth of what I have just claimed.

Yom Kippur calls upon us to recognize a radically different concept of marriage. Too much of our society has come to believe that marriage is about love and that it is only about love. Yom Kippur reminds us that it is also about a promise. Any two people can stay together as long as they both shall love each other. A marriage supposes that two people will stay together as long as they live. This sort of promise is not all that fashionable today. We have, in our culture, decided to make contracts instead of promises. What passes as a promise reads like a deal: "I will be there for you as long as you provide me with all the satisfaction that I have coming." This is not a promise; it is a contract. The difference is this: we keep promises even when we are not getting what we have coming. (The power of a promise is—in Stanley Hauerwa's words— "the power to stick with what we are stuck with.")

So you are attracted to someone else? Not receiving the love you deserve at home? You have needs? Welcome to the human race. "There is no true integrity without cost," writes Yale law professor Stephen Carter.

We are all human. We are frail. Lord knows we make mistakes. In moments of weakness we do not remember promises of Atonement Day. On this Day of Forgiveness, I do not ask nor do I expect perfection—and neither should anyone else. But, if a promise is anything, it is an indication of a determination to try.

Nobody knows what he or she is getting into when they get married. Nobody knows for sure what sort of person they will become. A man or a woman can become several different persons before a marriage is finished. One minister loudly proclaimed from the pulpit that his wife had slept with at least six different men since she had married him and each one of them was him. But, in one most important sense, we can stay the same person we were when we first got married: the person who makes and keeps the promise is always "the one who will be there" for the other.

I pause for a moment to offer praise and encouragement to those who sustain and nurture successful marriages—day by day, year by year. They see marriage as a sacred structure to be protected. They are committed to the marriage as well as to each other. They know that a successful marriage requires constant care and effort. They also know that while marriages may be made in heaven, all the maintenance work is done here on earth. I salute all who are sheltered and blessed by the sense of permanence they have created in their marriage.

Our families are an extension of that promise. What is a family but a community of promises made and promises kept—no matter what? A family is not just two or more people related by blood who happen to live under one roof. A family is not a management device by which two adults shuffle children around to the various experts who do the real rearing. A family is a community of people who dare to make a promise and care enough to keep it—no matter what. A real parent has the same name as God does: "Eheye asher eheye"—"I am the one who will be there with you."

A family is held together by promises: where promises fail, families fail. The rebirth of the family can begin only in the rebirth of promise keeping.

And if this commitment to promise keeping is a lifelong enterprise, we Jews have learned that it outlasts life itself. When death strikes, we come here to say Kaddish. Kaddish is really about keeping a promise. Death ends life, but it does not end a relationship, and we affirm that that relationship survives the grave. Kaddish is the way we honor our promises to our parents, even when they no longer walk this earth.

Thus, for us Jews, promises are a crucial dimension of our collective existence, the promise of the Jew to his God.

Unless we understand the crucial role which promises have played in Jewish thought, we cannot begin to understand Jewish history at all. If the Jew refused to be lured away from his ancestral faith, if he remained constant in the face of unspeakable cruelty and indescribable brutality, if he would not bend the knee before any earthly despots, it is because he believed in a God who was a "Zocher Ha-brith," one who would remember the promise. Then he, the Jew, had a promise to remember too. He had a task to perform, and he would not quit before he had seen it through.

For the heart of Jewish history is a promise—a promise renewed with every child that is born, with every Sabbath that is kept. "And the children of Israel shall keep the Sabbath, to observe the Sabbath throughout the generations, 'Brith Olam,' an everlasting promise." The Jew did not accept the cynical observation of Jonathan Swift that "promises and piecrusts are made to be broken." The promise was made to be kept. God would keep His promise to the Jew, and the Jew would keep his promise to God. And what is more, we have demonstrated convincingly that you can live on promises. We have done it.

Are we still true to the promise that we should remain faithful to God's mission for us?

In recent months, I came across an article with the title "Will Jews Become as Quaint as the Amish Are Today?" That item told of a poll by the *Los Angeles Times* which reported that 43 percent of American Jews said Jews should try to assimilate as much as possible into American society. Forty-one percent said Jews should try to maintain themselves as a distinctive group of Americans. And 16 percent were uncertain.

I recall a conversation that I had this year with a distinguished leader of the Roman Catholic Church. Engaged in dialogue, each of us spoke about the concerns we had for the welfare of the community of faith that each of us represented. The Catholic prelate spoke of his concern about the ascendancy of secularism, of material values, the stifling of the voice of the spirit. And I spoke about Jewish survival, my concern for the continuity of the Jewish faith in generations of the future. The cardinal was surprised, and he asked me to explain. I pointed out that there are one billion Catholics in the world and even if 10 percent chose a different religion or a different form of Christianity, the remaining numbers are so overwhelming that there would scarcely be a ripple in the Catholic community viewed as a whole. But if we of the Jewish community lost 10 percent year after year, one could see the demise of Judaism in a lifetime, God forbid. The cardinal smiled, and he said, "Don't worry, Rabbi, this will never happen because the Bible, which we both revere, abounds with God's promises that Israel will exist forever." An illustration. The prophet Malachi (3:6): "For I am God, I do not change; you are the children of Jacob, you will not cease to be." And then I was silent, savoring this extraordinary moment when a cardinal tells a rabbi not to worry about Jewish survival because the Torah tells us that God made a promise and God keeps His promises. But then I broke the silence, and I said the guarantee for survival is for the Jewish people as a nation. God's promise is that the people of Israel will exist forever. There are no guarantees for the individual Jew or a particular Jewish community.

Our task is to assure Jewish continuity where we are—in our homes, our families, our institutions. The challenge is daunting.

A harsh and caustic critic of American Jewry has made the following observation. American Jews, who are the most highly educated group in this country when it comes to general knowledge, are the least educated group when it comes to knowledge of their own heritage. We get our history from *Fiddler on the Roof,* our culture from Jackie Mason, our traditions from canned gefilte fish, our knowledge of the Bible from television, and our Jewish morality from Bible stories we learned as children. A portrait is a caricature, and his exaggerations are offensive, but there is a kernel of truth in his diatribe. How can we renew Jewish life and thereby fulfill the promise?

We know what is needed, and we know what works. Enhancing religious school education, particularly during the adolescent years; supporting Hillel Day School at this time of its dramatic growth as it projects its plan for a high school; supporting the Jewish theological seminary; providing Israel experiences for every teenager, Jewish family education, vibrant youth groups, Camp Ramah, Jewish summer camps for every child, and Hillel foundations on campuses throughout the country; and the list continues.

We witness today a new development. We are moving away from an image of Jewish education as schooling for children. What we see today is a remarkable reengagement of hundreds of thousands of Jews with the study of Torah. Adults are rediscovering the joys of serious Jewish study. Jewish education now extends beyond the classroom. We have come to understand that Jewish learning can take place in family education programs, in Chavurot, in the home, in the living room, in the office, in the corporate dining room, in the board room.

What a glorious opportunity is placed before all of us. Let it not be said of our generation that we were the most affluent Jewish community anywhere in the world but we were stricken by spiritual and intellectual poverty. Let it not be said of us that Judaism is rich and we are paupers. We have the capacity to fulfill the age-old promise to be a blessing to the world, the promise that has sustained us for four millennia.

A teenage student asked me recently, "Rabbi, are you aware that these are the last High Holidays of the twentieth century, that next year we shall celebrate Rosh Hashanah and Yom Kippur in the year 2000?" And he addressed me further and said, "What do you remember and know of the Jewish experience of the twentieth century?" That is another sermon, but I offer one word. When the State of Israel was first established, the chief rabbi of Israel wrote a prayer: "Our Father in Heaven, Rock and Redeemer of Israel, bless the State of Israel, the first flowering of our redemption." This century, out of terrifying death and darkness, we saw the first glimpse of the countenance of the Messiah: the resurrection of the Jewish people after the Holocaust, the reborn land of Israel, and our arrival in America. There should be no misunderstanding. The world is not perfect. Far, far from it. But never before in all of Jewish history have we had the power we now possess to bring healing, compassion, purpose, and peace to the world. "My generation witnessed the end of Jewish exile, the end of Jewish powerlessness and oppression. May yours witness the flowering of our redemption. But remember, you are part of a promise and that the Covenant is now handed to you."

On this Yom Kippur day we affirm that ours is a God of promises, a God Who has been there with us throughout our long history as a people. We pray that He will choose to be with us as we begin a new year, a new century, as we begin to forge a new Jewish future.

On this day, the Jewish people have gathered to affirm that we can create an identity for ourselves in relationship to each other, to our husbands, wives, to our children, to our community, to our parents, to ourselves.

On this Yom Kippur day, we have gathered to affirm that life begins and ends with those who dare to make a promise and care enough to keep the promises they make.

As we keep our promise to God, we merit His faithfulness to the promise we read every day of the year at morning services.

"And as for me, this is My Covenant with them, sayeth the Lord. My spirit which is upon you, and My words which I have put into your mouth, shall not depart from your mouth, nor from the mouth of your children, or from the mouth of your children's children, from this time and forever."

FAMILY

The Jew's home has rarely been his "castle"; throughout
the ages it has been something far higher—his sanctuary.
—RABBI JOSEPH H. HERTZ

I will walk within my house in the integrity of my heart.
—PSALM 101.2

The Jewish Family

On this Yom Kippur I share my concern about the Jewish family—an endangered species.

The Traditional Jewish Family

Consider what the Jewish family has been through the generations. One of the most profound contributions of Judaism to the human thought is the centrality of the home and the family. This is the cornerstone, the bulwark, and the bastion of our faith. The Jewish home is our impenetrable fortress. Tender are the bonds that bind the members of the family together.

The Jewish home was unique because it served as the first synagogue and the first school. The home was a synagogue, for in our tradition it is called a *Mikdash M'at*—a temple in miniature. The hearth of the home is its altar and the table its shrine. The father is the high priest, the mother high priestess, and the congregation their sons and daughters.

The key to understanding the Jewish home is contained in certain words. First, *sh'lom bayit*. If you achieve sh'lom bayit, you have life with contentment. Without sh'lom bayit, there are turmoil, conflict, and misery. Sh'lom bayit, which connotes a peaceful and wholesome

117

life, describes the serenity and beauty of family harmony based on love, responsibility, devotion, and care.

Another fundamental word is *Mishpachah.* Meaning far more than "family," it refers to the relationship of husband and wife; of parent and child; of grandparent and grandchild; of uncles, aunts, cousins, and even Machutanim.

The strength of the Jewish people has always been the Jewish family. No matter how burdened, oppressed, or battered by the winds of misfortune, the family has been the force that united our people. Caring one for the other in time of joy or sorrow, emotional interdependence, communication, a strong sense of values—these are some of the hallmarks of the Jewish family. It was the Jewish family that enabled the immigrant generation in the early period of the twentieth century, despite poverty and privation, to establish the foundation upon which the achievement of their children and grandchildren could be built.

Sam Levenson described his home as follows: "I was a most fortunate child. Ours was a home rich enough in family harmony and love to immunize eight kids against the potentially toxic effects of the environment beyond our door. Since the social scientists do not have a clinical name for the fortunate possessors of this kind of emotional security, I might suggest they label them 'The Privileged Poor.' Poverty never succeeded in degrading our family. We were independently poor."

Dore Schary once described his family. "In the Jewish life I knew there was a 'trinity' to whom we appealed or expressed our fears. A small accident would evoke 'mammenyu,' a larger mishap would bring forth 'tottenyu,' and shock would provoke 'Gottenyu.' A disaster could evoke an appeal to all three."

Mother, Father, and God represented the core of Jewish family life. Every home depended on the warmth and care given by Mother, the strength and security given by Father, and the omnipresence and omnipotence of God. Mother was there when you were ailing or hungry or cold, Father was always handy to protect you, and God was available for everything.

The Jewish Family Today

Today, we find a sense of uneasiness, a feeling that the great kind of family we Jews used to have is falling apart. We are not sure about our relationships with our spouses or theirs with us. We have guilt feelings toward our parents. We feel that somehow we and our children don't talk the same language and that we don't know where they are going. We suspect or at least we fear that they may be defecting from that long history to which we and they are heirs.

We used to boast that the Jewish home was a fortress against which hostile waves were beating in vain. The divorce rate among Jews was very low. Infidelity was rare. There was no drug problem. Alcoholism was virtually unknown among Jews. Intermarriage was kept to a low percentage. We do not say these things anymore, because they are not true any longer.

The influence of parents is in competition with other forces—the mass media; television; movies; the standards of the peer group; and the vague, yet pervasive, qualities of American mores. The traditional family was supported by a strong fabric of customs, standards, sanctions, and loyalties which is now rent at many points.

The traditional Jewish family had certain code words or phrases by which it resolved its tensions and differences and affirmed its values. One of these, that I do not hear anymore, is Derech Eretz, roughly translated as "respect" or "good manners." Every member of the family knew the meaning and overtones of the phrase. If a child acted brashly or inconsiderately, he needed no other reprimand to put him back on the right track; to recall a concept alone was sufficient. Every family member heard another phrase from time to time: "Es past nisht"—"This is not seemly or proper; this is something we don't do." We all knew this code language common to all members of the family which applied to siblings and parents and also the extended family.

Facts and Fallacies about the Family

Consider some of the facts and fallacies.

We assume that the traditional model of the nuclear family, the father as provider and the mother as homemaker and the children living at home, constitutes the majority of Jewish families. This model actually fits only a minority. For example, the large-scale entry of women into the world of work creates new child care requirements and demands new patterns for parenting. Husbands need to play a greater role as fathers of young children. Also, single parent families are an increasingly important aspect of our communal life. The sense of isolation and exclusion of these families should be overcome by understanding and concern.

We assume that the religious school or the day school can function in isolation from parents and grandparents and the family unit. This is not true. Without family involvement and participation, Jewish education will not touch the heart of the child.

The Congregational Family

The synagogue is not just a building for services and meetings, classes and activities. A congregation is, in an ideal sense, a family of families. We share joys and sorrows with each other. As our children become friends, we cherish the hope that someday they might be married to one another. We rejoice when they continue our loyalty and affiliation. A congregation is people with deep mutual loyalty sharing common memories with a sense of identification. If there was ever a need for creating this feeling of belonging and solidarity in the past, it is even greater now and will continue to grow in the future.

Sometime ago at the conclusion of a wedding ceremony which I performed, after I had pronounced the final benediction, the very nervous groom asked just loud enough for everyone to hear, "Are we finished?" "No," I declared. "You've just begun." Is the Jewish family finished?

No, we have just begun to examine new possibilities in the light of new conditions. But in the words of Pirke Avot, "The day is short and the work is great."

Our sages tell us that when God appeared to Moses, he spoke to him with the voice of his father. God always speaks to us through our parents. He speaks to our children with our voices. We are His representatives in their eyes. Let us be worthy of Him who sent us.

On Attaining Maturity

A braham is the subject of the Torah reading of both days of Rosh Hashanah. The rabbis of the Jewish tradition generally regarded him as the prototype of the perfect man. They therefore contemplated carefully every word in each passage which described his character. "And Abraham grew old and advanced in years." The Talmudic sages noted that in this verse, for the first time, there occurs a form of the word *Ziknah,* "old age." And so they constructed a fantastic legend around that word. They say, "Ad Avraham lo hayah ziknah"—"There was no old age until Abraham's time."

Despite the quaint and exotic character of their comment, they seek to convey a profound truth, for they impart to us the insight that people may live long without growing old, that maturity is not a matter of years. "Yesh lecha adam she-hu b'zik-nah v'ayno b'yamim, b'yamim v'ayno b'ziknah"—"There are people who grow up though not old, and others who grow old but do not grow up."

All of us want the fulfillment of life's promise. Some are kept from it by limitations of birth, or ability, or illness, or other circumstance. But most of us are denied the realization of our dreams because of something within ourselves.

A major part of our difficulty with life springs from our failure to grow up. There are multitudes who go through life with the physical proportions of manhood or womanhood and with the immature and infantile ways of children. Some of us may grow to a man's size and yet feel or think like children. Childish minds are dangerous when they are housed in adult bodies. They have the power to put immaturity into effect. A recent observer has claimed that "immaturity stands out as the number one troublemaker in bringing about mental, emotional, and social ills." Immaturity produces a painful harvest—divorce, broken homes, estrangement of parents and children, drug abuse, delinquency, violence, fear, and hatred.

As we enter a New Year we should ask ourselves the question found in the prayer book: "What are we, what is life?" Am I only a year older, or am I also a year wiser? Have I grown and matured, or have I taken another step in the direction of foolishness? A sign in the office of a business executive reads, "If you could kick the person responsible for most of your troubles, you wouldn't be able to sit for six months."

I recently had occasion to measure my son David, who celebrated his Bar Mitzvah last November, against the yardstick to see how much he had grown. It is an exciting moment. But we adults stop doing that when we reach the limits of our physical size, as though the exhilaration of growth is no longer possible to us, as if there is nothing left to grow toward any more.

But maturity is not a one-time achievement. It is a process that ends only with death. The acquisition of maturity is always relative. No one can say, "I am mature." The most we can hope is that we shall continue to mature.

What is maturity? There is a certain ambiguity in the use of the term which creates confusion. Today's advisers to the perplexed, upon whom so many have come to rely so heavily, assure us that anyone who strays from the path of marital fidelity is "immature." But on another page of the newspaper we find that certain movies and novels are described as "mature" because they treat such lapses graphically, tolerantly, even admiringly. "Mature" does not mean sophisticated.

Also, the rabbis emphasized that age is not to be identified with maturity. In the Bible, God's prophets are often portrayed as being

comparatively young. Amos, Hosea, and Jeremiah, among others, delivered their most fateful messages as young men. One encounters adults
who remain in a state of perpetual childishness and young people who
possess wisdom far beyond their years.

In a novel by Louis Broomfield, the leading character reflects upon
the meaning of his life in the following way: "But with me there was no
growth. There was no creation. In all my life there had never been,
until I was near to middle age, either the necessity or the desire to
think. Really to think is not a simple thing. It cannot easily be taught,
and learning by experience requires time and a steadily growing maturity. I had already lost nearly twenty years which should have been
employed in thinking, and because those years had been wasted I had
never attained any degree of maturity. I had merely grown older, and
like those men who constantly cling to their youth or return to it at college reunions and Legion conventions, I had merely withered."

Maturity may be defined as a measure of the quality of our relationships and of the way in which we live them.

We need some kind of standard by which to evaluate the part which
we play in the network of relationships and linkages that comprises our
existence. The insights of psychology and the perspectives of religion
achieve fruitful union in the establishment of a set of criteria to guide
us in living. On this day of the New Year, a time when we seek personal
renewal by accurate self-assessment, let us examine important guides
for responsible living.

First, however, a word of warning. The following guides of maturity
may seem like counsels of perfection, but they should not be viewed as
such. They are navigational aids, as it were, to help us move through the
uncertain and ever-changing waters of life. Also, the speaker who offers
them does not claim to fulfill them in greater measure than those to
whom his words are addressed.

1. The first criterion is self-acceptance. Self-esteem and self-appreciation are not only legitimate, they are desirable. You are your first best
friend, and you may also be your worst enemy. People who hate them-

selves, who are always wishing that they were somewhere else or someone else, that they had been born at a different time—these people are
doing violence to themselves and to life. The mature person is not self-
pitying, self-denying, or self-excusing. Nor is he or she overly assertive
and belligerent. Until a person learns to accept and help himself, he
cannot be a full human being. The ethics of the fathers taught, "Be not
wicked in your own estimation." Do not be afraid of being labeled as a
narcissist or of being charged with self-love. There is a self-love which
is destructive, but there is a self-love which is affirmative, constructive,
and necessary for health. The mature person is not self-pitying, nor is
he so self-deprecating that he fails to undertake those efforts of which
he is capable.

2. The mature person is able to accept things and people the way
they are rather than pretend they are the way he wants them to be.

Children lead a rich fantasy life. Mature people are capable of imagination, or flights of fancy, but they take up their permanent residence
in the world of fact. They live by the reality principle. The immature are
not necessarily mentally disturbed, but they still look at life from an
essentially childish level, moving back and forth between fantasy and
reality, fiction and truth. The mature person keeps his vision fresh and
his mind alert, avoiding clichés, stereotypes, and unfounded general-
izations. People who are prejudiced are emotionally immature. They
are so comfortable with their false images of the world that they cannot
bear to part with them.

The more mature we are, the more we are able to see things as they
are and to act accordingly. Quite often I am asked whether a child as
young as six or seven should attend a funeral service of someone who
was dear to him. My answer generally is yes. I stress the child's need to
face up to reality from the beginning. I believe that children need to
participate in human experiences rather than to be carried along in a
succession of mysteries that may prevent them from seeing the world
with wide open eyes.

The prophet Ezekiel heard a divine command: "Stand on thy feet, son of man, and I will speak unto thee." God speaks to men who stand on their feet, head erect, facing life with composure and faith.

3. We are mature to the extent that we are guided by our long-term purposes rather than by our immediate desires.

When we were children, feelings often determined our actions. We were emotional, and our behavior was often irrational. As we grew older, we began to acquire some ability to discipline our feelings, to control our actions according to enduring and significant goals. The Bible says of Moses, "Va-yigdal Moshe"—"And Moses grew up"; "Va-yetze el echov"—"And he went forth unto his brethren." He went beyond the claims of self-interest, beyond the pleasures of the palace, beyond the comforts of high status. He sent his mind and his heart forth on an expedition into society. He lived in terms of a great ideal to free his brethren from the yoke of their bondage.

Each of us, as we enter maturity, can define for ourselves those goals and purposes which will give us the power to rise above the pursuit of pleasure for more lasting values. This does not mean that we should not have our moments of ease or of relaxation or of unburdened escape. But it does mean that we must be able to measure the temporary pleasures of the moment against the permanent satisfactions of a lifetime. The more mature we become, the more we appreciate Plato's insight that we must become experts in the art of measurement. We have to weigh a future pleasure against a present pain and a present pleasure against a future pain.

The ethics of the fathers advise every man that he should conduct his life with a full awareness of three principles: "Know whence you come, where you are going, and before whom you will some day submit a reckoning." A mature existence is lived by those who seek more than creature comforts and self-indulgence as they aspire to the abiding values of faith, goodness, and beauty.

4. Responsibility. The human being is born irresponsible. He did not choose to enter the human scene, and for a long time after his entrance

he is helpless to do much about it. Yet, if we hear a grown man justify his lack of responsible participation by saying that after all he didn't ask to be born, we can set him down as immature. He overlooks the simple fact that nobody else did either. To be mature is to accept the fact that human experience is a shared experience; a person remains immature whatever his age as long as he thinks of himself as an exception to the human race. Mature responsibility involves a willing participation in the chores of life and a creative participation in the enhancement of life. Abraham is the prototype of maturity for he is the man who assumes responsibility not only for himself, for his family, and for the future of his faith but even for the wicked cities of Sodom and Gomorrah.

An employer once interviewed an applicant for a position, and he said to the candidate, "For this job I want a responsible man." The applicant announced, "Then you want me. Everywhere I worked when something went wrong they said I was responsible." We are as mature as the responsibilities we dare accept. We are as large as the task we are willing to undertake and to carry through. Arthur Miller, in a very moving drama, put these words in the mouth of one of his characters: "It's not your guilt I want—it's your responsibility."

5. The mature person accepts his heritage. As a Jew, he does not waste his life bemoaning his allegedly unfortunate status. Jean-Paul Sartre, the French philosopher, once pointed out that Jews have a common bond that transcends the religious, cultural, national, or ethnic. They have one thing in common—their situation. The only question that the individual faces is his freedom to answer the question of what kind of a Jew he shall be. Shall he rebel against it, deny it, or attempt to escape it? This is, in the words of the philosopher, the "inauthentic Jew." Or shall he accept it and assume the responsibilities this identity imposes and live as happily, as gracefully, and meaningfully as he can? This is what the authentic Jew does. He draws from his Jewish identity sources of meaning and inspiration that enrich his life and broaden his interests. As a consequence the mature Jew has an enlarged self. The Jewish ego is stretched to include the tears of oppressed slaves, the

thoughts of majestic sages, the ideals of prophets and rabbis. Through the study of the Torah, the centuries rolled through the mind of the Jew, and he became the contemporary of saints. Through the insistence of Judaism that its followers should remember that they should never separate themselves from the needy or from the hungry, they were made citizens of the universe. The whole world of humanity entered the heart of the educated Jew.

6. A mature person is one who is able to accept his own and the opposite sex and the relation between the two in ways that are appropriately fulfilling. In a word, it is important for a man to be happy because he is a man and for a woman to be happy because she is a woman. In our society neither one is simple. It has been stated, "In our civilization men are afraid that they will not be men enough, and women are afraid that they might be considered only women." This latter concern has been one of the forces for the women's liberation movement, united under a banner demanding social equality with men, equal pay, equal educational opportunities, and emancipation from those inequities with which women have suffered since time immemorial. That these demands are valid is undeniable. But sometimes one wonders about the harsh and strident tone of some of the statements issued by the extremists in this movement. There are men who want to reject the masculine role, and increasingly one senses that there are women who want to do the same because of their less favored position. The emotionally mature man does not wish to escape his manliness, but he does not necessarily identify such manliness with power or dominance, for he has the capacity for tenderness and sensitivity in his relationships with wife and child. The woman discovers in her sex, without surrendering her rights of equality or autonomy, unique satisfactions and experiences. Each of us rejoices in what he is and has and looks for her complement in the other.

7. The mature person is able to achieve a balance between work and leisure. He is able to work without being a slave and to play without

feeling that he ought to be working. Labor is a basic element in a fulfilling life. The first and greatest worker in the world was God Himself, the Creator of heaven and earth. It was He who set the pattern for man in the six days of creation as well as the Sabbath which followed. When we describe an occupation as a calling or use its Latin equivalent "vocation," we are being reminded that each of us in his labor is answering a call from God to share with Him in building the world. "Avodah" means both labor and worship.

But the mature person also knows how to detach himself from his work and, with a sense of relief and liberation, give himself to recreation. He is able to use his leisure to widen his interests and activities, to undergo new experiences, to widen the horizons of his mind, and occasionally to be with himself. It is not a mark of wisdom for a man to spend seventy to eighty hours a week in his business or profession. Achieving a harmonious balance between labor and rest is an essential ingredient of maturity.

8. The mature person is one who is able to love others so well that he becomes less dependent on being loved. This sounds like a simple prescription. It is perhaps the most difficult of all tasks. We use the word *love* in the broad sense of true friendliness with other human beings, of considering the interests of other individuals.

Probably the most significant cause of unhappiness is the incapacity to give affection to others. Psychologists have recognized stages in the emotional development of humanity. The infant is characterized by the almost incessant use of the word *me*—"Give *me*," "*Me* no like." Notice how often an infant has its little fist closed as a kind of physical symbol of this identification of everything with its little "me." As reason begins to unfold the pronoun *me* is changed to *I*. The highest stage is attained when one moves from the "me" and the "I" to the "thou" or the love of neighbor: "And thou shalt love thy neighbor as thyself." That "thou" is understood as a person of worth bearing within himself the divine image, endowed with those qualities which make him a child of God. The neighbor is not necessarily the one close to me. The neighbor is whoever happens to cross my path at any moment. The neighbor is not always someone we like—he could just as well be someone we do not like—and yet we are under the commandment to love. Spiritual maturity is reached when we love each "thou" that we meet with something of the same love we bear ourselves, pardoning when he does wrong, praising when he does right, finding excuses in the same way we excuse ourselves.

Love is more than the ideal of the romantic. Love is relatedness. Man is a lonely creature in a hostile world. Love is the key which opens the doors of his prison and releases him from confinement. He can then go forth to enjoy the wonder of nature, the companionship of his kind, and the fellowship of society. Through love he overcomes his apartness. "Love or perish," says modern psychology. The Jewish sages said it better, "Companionship or death."

Can maturity, as judged by these standards, be attained? Is there hope for the realization of a mature life? Abraham achieved maturity. So did the prophets, the sages, and the rabbis of old who mastered childish impulses and infantile desires as they built the foundations of an enduring and life-sustaining faith.

Most men and women have a deep urge to grow up, to secure the unique privileges of a responsible adulthood. The world needs more healthy-minded, independent, self-reliant, reality-oriented spirits than ever before. As we pray for life, let us pray that we not only grow older but wiser. May we, like Abraham, acquire insight into ourselves so that we find the greatest satisfaction not in wanting everything, as a child desires everything that glitters, but in knowing what we really want. Each of us needs more self-awareness, more self-mastery, more inner stability. In the coming year, may we all move in the direction of greater maturity so that, like Abraham, we can achieve the blessings with which his life was crowned—"Zaken ve-savea"— "ripeness of years, satisfaction, and fulfillment."

Love: A Jewish Definition

At this season, I shall discuss one of the most sacred and yet misused words of our time. It bounces around in conversations, group discussions, sermons, and other exhortations, meaning many different things to different people. The word is *love*.

I suggest that we endeavor to clarify it because I believe that, in many respects, love—as concept, standard, and ideal—is at the very heart of the significance of these Yomim Noraim—Days of Awe.

The character of that love is expressed many times in the prayer book, in our liturgy, and in the symbols and practices of this High Holiday season. What are the two great imperatives of Judaism? "Thou shalt love the Lord thy God with all thy heart and with all thy soul and with all thy might" and "Thou shalt love thy neighbor as thyself."

These texts cry out for interpretation. Since love is an emotion, how can it be commanded? How can feelings become duties? What is the authentic biblical conception of love? Let us examine the context.

"Thou shalt love the Lord thy God with all thy heart . . ." What follows? "Thou shalt teach these words to thy children. Thou shalt talk of them when thou sittest in thy house, when thou walkest by the way, when thou liest down and when thou risest up, thou shall bind them for a sign upon thy hand. They shall be for frontlets between thine eyes. Thou shalt write them upon the doorposts of thy house and upon thy gates."

The love of God is not a security blanket, a warm puppy, or a kind of vapid sentimentality. It requires the fulfillment of obligations, the performance of deeds, the faithful assumption of duties. These include teaching our children, bearing witness to God's word, offering to Him our prayers, affixing the mezuzah, donning tefillin, responding to His commands.

A mother once overheard her little boy's prayer in which he listed the many things he wanted the Almighty to deliver to him, preferably before the weekend. She interrupted his prayers by remarking, "Don't give God so many orders. Just report for duty."

The imperative to love in the Sh'ma is immediately identified with the acceptance of duty and obligation.

What about the commandment to love one's neighbor? This is stated in the nineteenth chapter of the Book of Leviticus, verse 18. The chapter itself deals with the following precepts: consideration for the needy, prompt wages for reasonable hours, no talebearing or malice, dealing honorably, cordiality and sympathy for the alien and the stranger, consideration for the poor, equal justice for the rich and the poor, and the prohibition of hatred and vengeance.

To love thy neighbor in the biblical sense does not mean to become romantically involved with him. Of course, love is connected with deep emotional levels of human existence. But the love that is here stated is not an emotion, or else how could it be commanded?

What the Bible and the later rabbinic sources defined as "Ahavat Habriyot," love of one's fellow man, is spelled out in the duties demanded of us: fidelity, kindness, humanity, brotherliness. You must do for your neighbor what you expect him to do for you: respect him, sympathize with him, receive him kindly, judge him favorably, aid him in his distress, help him at the cost of sacrifice to yourself.

Love is not an occasional impulse but a compelling duty that should be expressed in deeds continually and consistently.

A puzzled doctor was unable to diagnose his patient's symptoms. He finally called the man's wife. "I must tell you that your husband says that the first time he kisses you, he feels very warm. Then, the next time he kisses you, he is chilled and shivering with cold. Can you give me an explanation?" "There's nothing strange about it," the wife replied. "The first time he kisses me, it's August; the next time, it's February."

A very important truth emerges from these texts. Love is responsibility. Responsibility is an entirely voluntary act. The loving person responds, for he feels responsible for his fellow man as he feels responsible for himself.

Most of us identify love with a feeling or an emotion. One falls in love, one falls out of love, in uneven rhythms. Feelings are pendulums. They swing up or down depending upon such unstable things as the barometer, the digestion, the time of the month, or the side of the bed out of which we crawl on a given morning. Feelings are notoriously fickle and unstable. It follows that people who identify love with feelings become inconstant lovers. I therefore suggest that love, as Judaism views it, is an activity, not a passive emotion. It's a verb, not a noun. Love is primarily giving, not receiving.

The Siddur declares, "Ahavah Rabah." God has shown great love for the Jewish people. He demonstrates it by giving us the Torah, His most supremely cherished possession.

It is possible to give without loving. We have that experience on April 15 of every year. But one can't experience love without giving. What can we give to God? The best of our heart and mind and soul. What are we commanded to give him? An entire way of life.

Consider a different text found in Jewish folk culture in an American adaptation, *Fiddler on the Roof:* that well-known passage when Tevye discovers that his daughter, Hodel, is marrying for love, something unheard of in Anatevka. He turns to Golda, his wife, and he asks her, "Do you love me?" And she says, "You're a fool."

"I know, but do you love me?"

"Do I love you? For twenty-five years, I have washed your clothes, cooked your meals, cleaned your house, given you children, milked the cow. After twenty-five years, why talk about love right now?"

Tevye is not satisfied. He turns to her and repeats the question, "Do you love me?"

"I'm your wife."

"I know—but do you love me?"

"Do I love him? For twenty-five years, I've lived with him, fought with him, starved with him. For twenty-five years my bed is his. If that's not love, what is?" Does she answer the question which he asks her four times? It seems as though she doesn't, for she responds by asking him questions. But we know that she has answered him and that she loves him. For love, as it has been said, is what you've been through with somebody. Love doesn't make the world go round. Love is what makes the ride worthwhile.

A husband who does not show any responsibility for his wife doesn't really love her. A wife who does not offer care and concern for her husband does not really love him. Parents who are unconcerned about the welfare of their children do not love them. The test of love is the level of responsibility that we are ready to accept because of it. A young man who seemingly "fell in love" sent a letter to his girlfriend: "I will climb the highest mountain for you. I will traverse the trackless desert for you. I will journey across the greatest ocean for you. P.S. I'll see you on Saturday night, if it doesn't rain."

What troubles me as I seek to interpret love and responsibility? I shall speak plainly. Some people think of love as the exchange of two momentary desires in the contact of two skins. That is a definition at the opposite end of the Jewish view, for that is narcissism masquerading as love.

It would be easy, too easy, to talk about the casual attitude toward sexual relationships that is so evident in our time; to refer to the decline in those moral standards that have characteristically guided the Jewish marriage and home; and to issue a sweeping condemnation of those who violate the most sacred and hallowed of covenants, the bond of marriage. But to do that would be to avoid the more difficult task, which is to explore why people fail to achieve authentic love and why they slide into that which is unworthy, profane, and demeaning.

In the film *Butterflies Are Free?* a superficial, scatterbrained girl, played by Goldie Hawn, is portrayed in the act of running away from her blind lover. She explains her flight and justifies it by shouting at him, "Because you're blind. You're crippled."

In the most profound moment of the movie, the young man replies, "No, I'm not crippled. I'm sightless but not crippled. You are crippled because you cannot commit yourself to anyone."

That is the test of love. That is the requirement of love. Commitment of the responsible self which endures to sustain a relationship of trust and faith is the sign of authentic love.

Becoming a whole person must include not just what one can have and can enjoy but equally the continuing relationships and abiding commitments through which alone one can mature. True friendship increases in time both in understanding and in demand. True love deepens to obligate us as well as to quicken us over the years. These are what make us fully human. Marriage and a family involve profound commitment and unsullied trust. Of course, it's difficult to become fully human. But the wisdom of the centuries instructs us that this goal is worthy of our highest striving.

Our hedonistic culture suggests that to love means to have fun. Everything should be tried, and sex is no different from travel, or restaurants, or skin diving. This is the sophisticated attitude of our time.

That is not what the Jewish faith terms love. The love that is consecrated in Judaism requires a high standard of personal discipline, for intimacy and fidelity mean that we are engaged in the loving service of the other, a service that sometimes demands from the other, sometimes consoles and reassures. The sensitivity, the perseverance, the wit, the tenderness, the compassion, and the strength that are necessary for such loving service do not come naturally or easily to the human species. We learn by trial and error, by practice, and by help from those we love.

It is important to note that we do not live in a world that is anywhere near perfect. Human relationships go on in a context of headaches, sick children, sudden interruptions, exhausting days, late airplanes, cars that won't start, children to be chauffeured, bills to be paid, and jobs to be done. In the midst of all these demands, distractions, and frustrations, the development and nurture of intimacy and fidelity require responsibility. He who does not understand that truth will either learn it the hard way or will never learn anything at all about human relationships.

I once came upon a comment that an archaeologist makes the best husband any woman can have. The older she gets, the more interested he is in her. There's more than a touch of cynicism in that remark. I prefer a different formulation of marriage. "Marriage is that relationship between man and woman in which the independence is equal, the dependence mutual, and the obligation reciprocal."

A word about the love of parents and children. Love means the affirmation, not the possession, of the one loved. Responsibility can easily deteriorate into domination and possessiveness. It is therefore important to indicate that love is the active concern for the life and growth of those whom we love. We are concerned that the other should grow and unfold for his or her own sake and in his or her own way. Here too, the Jewish view demands responsive love expressed in discipline and devotion. Here, too, a covenant is made between the generations in which there are reciprocal obligations which enable spiritual and personal growth to be nurtured and fulfilled.

Do we love the Jewish people? We have yet to overcome the divisiveness and separation that persist in Jewish life today.

The Hasidic master Raphael of Bershad was about to set out on a journey. A number of his followers decided to go along, and they sat down in the wagon with him. As they were about to depart, yet another student said he wanted to join them, but the other students protested, saying the coach was already too crowded. Listening to the exchange, the master said, "Then we will just have to love each other that much more."

One Jewish group is accused of willfully splitting the Jewish people. Another group is caricatured as being repressive. Still another is fanatical. Still another is too "dovish" and does not provide for Israel's security. Yet another is indecisive. If we are to journey together as one people, we shall have to love each other more.

Jewish life in the Diaspora is divided among the streams of Orthodox, Conservative, Reform, and others. One often hears intergroup rejection and denunciation. To the innuendoes and thinly veiled hostility, we should say, "Enough!" We should devote ourselves to dialogue and mutual exploration. We should learn to tone down the vituperative rhetoric, while not abandoning our individual Jewish commitments. We should break down the stereotypes that divide us from each other. Through our openness, we should restore civility to intra-Jewish dialogue.

What we need now, more than ever, is what Rabbi Abraham Isaac Kook, of an earlier generation, practiced: "Ahavat Chinom,"—"love of our fellow Jews," even if we disagree with them, even if we oppose their views. We are to be affectionate to leaders and spokesmen even if such affection does not seem warranted. Someone asked Rabbi Kook, "Aren't there some Jews who are not deserving of that?" And he answered, "If I have to make a mistake, let my mistake be that I loved a Jew who didn't deserve to be loved."

We who have instructed the world in the tragic lessons of Auschwitz need to instruct ourselves. In the darkest hour of Jewish life, while the enemy howled, we knew we had each other. It was our comfort and our strength. We were one people, with one fate and one destiny.

What is demanded of every Jew and every movement is basic respect for other schools of thought. In a deeper sense, we should strive for more than respect. Jews need each other's uniqueness. We need to hear each other's *niggun*, the melody that each group sings. We need the diversity that helps us to find our way on the path that leads to Jewish loyalty and pride. We need to put the welfare of Klal Yisrael—the totality of the Jewish people—ahead of other considerations.

The second manifestation of love is memory. I recognize a great fellowship, the fellowship of the bereaved. Many of us have loved and lost. The death of a loved one leaves gaping holes in our lives, feelings of loneliness and emptiness, sometimes of bitterness. Love strengthens our will to remember. Because of the memory, as long as we live, our departed will live, for they are part of us.

When we are weary and in need of strength, we remember them.

When we have joys that we crave to share, we remember them. When we have decisions difficult to make, we remember them. When we have achievements based on their guidance, we remember them. When we are weak, the recollection of their courage can give us strength. When we are perplexed, the memory of their understanding will give us insight. When we are discouraged, the memory of their resolution and faith will give us hope.

Those of us who have lost loved ones have learned in our sorrow that we pay an enormous price for love when it ceases to flow. We pay in the coin of grief, longing, yearning, missing. It hurts so much. Whenever we love someone, we offer a hostage to fortune. Whenever we permit someone to become very dear to us, we become vulnerable to disappointment and heartbreak.

What, then is our choice? Never permit ourselves to love anyone? Never permit anyone to matter to us? Deny ourselves the greatest of all God-given joys?

If loving is expensive, being unloved and unloving costs even more. I believe that even in our grief, we can still agree with the sentiment of a contemporary writer: "To love and be loved is to feel the sun from both sides."

Great love stories have no endings. Have we stopped loving our departed ones? Do we forget them? Of course, we are not enslaved to the past, and the stream of activity moves us forward, and we cherish life in the present. But within the texture of our lives are woven the personalities of those whom we have loved and lost.

May the New Year bring us many gifts. But may the greatest of them all be the love that enables us to assume responsibility for ourselves, for those who need us, for our departed, for our people, for all mankind. It is in this loving service that our most cherished blessings will be found.

How to Be a Mentsch

In the course of these days, we shall address our concern for the redemption of the Jewish people, for the synagogue, for Soviet Jewry, for Israel, for the Jewish home, for the Jewish community. But today, I would like to focus on what Judaism has to say to each of us about finding meaning, about selfhood. How do I find a way that will enable me to live out my life with all my heart, with all my soul, with all my might, without a hiding place, without retreat?

When we look at the text or we listen to the scholars, the answer is, "Study; learn; attend a school; become a master of the text." And we believe in the power of learning. That is why 85 percent of our youngsters who are eligible are in college, four hundred thousand in all. That is why 10 percent of the college faculty members in this country and 20 percent in the elite institutions are Jews. But that is not what the rabbis had in mind by study. The great sages also asked, "Tachlis?"—"What for?" And that is why we are taught: "If somebody studies not for the purpose of doing good, it would be better if he were not born." Why? Is this not strange for people with such intellectual history as ours?

I am reminded of a true story about a nice Jewish boy. His name is Eric Breindel. He graduated Phi Beta Kappa and magna cum laude from Harvard University. He is the embodiment of every Jewish mother's dream. It gets better. He graduated from Harvard Law

School, very near the top of his class. He became a staff member of Senator Daniel Patrick Moynihan's select committee on the intelligence program of the United States.

Samuel Pisar mentions Breindel in his book *Of Blood and Hope,* crediting him as an extremely bright young man, a "comer," with an uncanny ability to get things done.

All of this is at the tender age of twenty-nine, a phenomenal success. Would any of our children grow up like him? Right? Not exactly right.

What I did not mention was that on May 23, 1984, he was arrested for buying five packets of heroin from an undercover agent in a Holiday Inn in Washington, D.C. He was convicted and removed from his congressional post. He has been sentenced, and he has been disbarred from the legal profession. His life, of infinite potential, has been wasted.

The intellect alone is not sufficient to guide us in answering the ultimate question that challenges us on this day.

The answer lies in a Yiddish word. I hope it is familiar, one of the most beautiful and evocative words in the Yiddish language. A word with many associations and which conveys a unique sensibility. The word is *mentsch.* It means "a person," but it means much more. *Mentsch* means "an ideal human being." It means a person who has cultivated a character of sensitivity, of dignity, of care and compassion.

What is missing? "Mentschlichkeit." We can produce the best lawyers, the most talented doctors, the most astute business executives, the most talented professionals, the most capable career specialists. But if we don't instill mentschlichkeit, there will be more Eric Breindels— not as extreme, not as tragic, not as catastrophic. But without mentschlichkeit, there can be no authentic, enduring, and meaningful success in the act of living.

At a conference for child care professionals and educators, the renowned psychologist Dr. Jerome Bruner cautioned all parents with these words: "I think parents should forget the 'genius' bit—what you want is a human being, a mentsch, not a genius."

The Jewish folk tradition offered a commentary on the meaning and implication of being a mentsch.

When a person failed to perform the basic acts demanded by an elemental sense of decency, it was a source of shock and consternation. When asked about such a person, the question was phrased, What happened to his mentschlichkeit?—What happened to his humanity?

Our people knew the reality of human imperfection, and therefore they said, "A mentsch iz nit kein malach"—"A person is not an angel." Even the best of us is frail and weak, and we often sin and make mistakes.

We recall how our patriarch, Jacob, deceived his blind father, Isaac, in order to acquire his brother's birthright. He committed a great sin, which the Torah does not attempt to hide. Ultimately, he engaged in a mysterious struggle with an angel. Jacob was victorious in that struggle, but he emerged from the battle limping. Perhaps the meaning of that battle is that Jacob had to struggle with himself to overcome his own sinfulness. He had to struggle to become a mentsch. He did not emerge unscathed. And each of us is Jacob.

A mentsch is not an angel. We Jews do not expect perfection of any person, even of one who becomes a real mentsch. But each of us must enter the fray to try to become a mentsch.

If you want to write a best seller, write a book entitled *How to Lose Weight while Eating Ice Cream* or *How to Look Younger Each Day of Your Life* or *How to Find Health, Wealth, and Happiness in Ten Days.*

But if somebody decided to write a book entitled *How to Be a Mentsch,* I doubt it would cause a great stir. But the book, the tradition that addresses this theme, is the Torah.

How do we teach mentschlichkeit? How do we acquire it? How do we transmit it?

The answer lies with the observances and practices and disciplines of Judaism, with the way of Torah, but not Torah restricted to an abstract intellectual exercise but Torah as a way of life.

We fix a mezuzah to the door and thereby declare that our home is a holy place, a sanctuary in which integrity, love, and responsibility are to be taught and practiced.

Even the food we eat testifies to our reverence for life. We do not kill animals wantonly. We make of our table an altar.

Every Sabbath day that we keep declares that we reject commerce as having absolute control over our lives. We enjoy a tranquility of the spirit and inner peace that are linked with faith and worship.

When we fast on Yom Kippur, we experience a sense of repentance in our physical being as well as in our words, and we feel the pain of the hungry and the deprived, and we are stirred, in the words of the prophet, to "unlock the fetters of wickedness," to let the oppressed go free, and to share our bread with the hungry.

Ours is a society where everything is in a state of constant flux. There are no more certainties; no permanent values; sometimes, I think, no enduring relationships. As a result, we find ourselves in a state of spiritual chaos and confusion. Too many of our best and brightest lose their way.

But we Jews have a tradition that is four thousand years old. From our historic experience, we have achieved profound insights and great wisdom embodied in the values taught and preserved by our heroes and heroines and by our great books. These values are not disposable like yesterday's newspaper. They are values by which it is possible for a human being to live a meaningful life in the last decades of the twentieth century.

These values have one goal. It is to try to make a mentsch out of each one of us. Because if you are a mentsch, our tradition says, you can be relied upon under all circumstances. You can be a mentsch for all seasons. If you are a student, you will resist the pressure of others who want you to take drugs, to get high, to use sex as a substitute for love. If you are a mentsch and you have a profession, your concern for your client or your patient will supersede your concern for your own self-aggrandizement. If you are a mentsch and you are in business, your concern for integrity will not be compromised by your desire for profits.

If you are a mentsch and there is a crisis, you will be the person who can be counted upon to help others as well as yourself.

Rabbi Leo Baeck was a distinguished Reform rabbi in Berlin before the Second World War. In 1938 and 1939, when he was almost seventy years old, he was offered the pulpit of a large congregation in Cincinnati. But he refused to leave his people in Germany. He made many trips between Berlin and London to make arrangements for Jewish-German children to stay in Britain. Ultimately, he was imprisoned by the Nazis in the concentration camp Theresienstadt. There, by day, he had to drag a garbage cart along the street. But at night, Rabbi Baeck would give illegal lectures to fellow Jews on philosophy, literature, and Jewish history. In total darkness, eight hundred to nine hundred people would crowd into the attic of a barracks to listen to his teaching. In the midst of hunger, disease, and torture, he was able to give courage to his people by teaching them every night. Whenever he could steal a moment from his forced labor, he would write on tiny scraps of paper what was ultimately to become a profound psychological history of the Jewish people. He would then read from those scraps of paper to his fellow Jews, thereby giving them the will to survive. "A mentsch remains a mentsch, even in Theresienstadt."

A mentsch has the capacity to love, to give, to share, and to nurture because he has achieved self-acceptance and self-appreciation. "Love your neighbor as yourself" is a moral statement that conveys a profound psychological truth. People who don't like themselves don't like others. People who like themselves don't think about themselves. They think about the world. They think about other people.

A mentsch understands that when a person authentically loves his neighbor, he is strengthened by the very act of giving and relating to others.

To be a mentsch means to give and to draw satisfaction from and to find joy in giving. A noted student of human behavior underlined this truth: "Not he who has much is rich, but he who gives much. The hoarder, who is anxiously worried about losing something, is the poor, impoverished man, regardless of how much he has. Whoever is capable of giving of himself is rich."

To be a mentsch means to give of our means and to give of ourselves. It means comforting the bereaved, visiting the sick, transcribing braille for the blind, settling the stranger in our midst, working on behalf of Soviet Jewry, lending a hand to the synagogue, to the community, to the causes and movements that need our help. We call these deeds of "G'Milut Chassadim"—"loving-kindness." They heal not only the object of such goodness but also those who perform such generous deeds, because those who engage in G'Milut Chassadim transform not only the situation but also their own character.

A glorious God gave each of us a treasure, a precious gift—a *Neshama*, a soul—and we can find it by linking it to the world out there that has to be saved and redeemed. There is something specific and particular that every one of us can do, something we can do with our very being, with our care, with our intelligence, with our unique spirit.

How do we answer the question, Where are you? Who are you? Each of us is a human being on the path of becoming a mentsch. And mentschlichkeit can transform our lives and the world in which we live. Try to be the kind of person who will be respected and loved not because of power, fame, success, or fortune, but because you personify the qualities of mentschlichkeit—because you are fair, generous, caring, and compassionate under all circumstances. To be a mentsch is a challenge issued to each of us. May we be strengthened, encouraged, and guided as we meet that challenge and thereby bring blessing to the world and to ourselves.

FREEDOM

History proves that, with all the set-backs and backslidings, America has come through its trials and tribulations, often scarred but always strengthened and prepared to carry on the glory of its adventures in freedom.

—RABBI SOLOMON D. GOLDFARB

Proclaim liberty throughout the land unto all the inhabitants thereof.

—LEVITICUS 25.10

A New Contract

The Question We Face

When we arrived in this country in our masses, the basic tactic we employed in our effort to gain admission into American society was to deny that we were in any significant way different from everybody else. The Jew believed he was offered a contract: American citizenship in exchange for Jewishness, freedom for accommodation. He accepted it eagerly. So thoroughly did he convince his son and daughter there were no differences between Jews and other Americans, so assiduously did he establish institutions of Americanization, that it is no surprise to find that his children believed him. Since Jews have been committed so passionately to the idea of equality, their children ask, "Why do you insist that we remain religiously and ethnically separate?"

We are faced with an agonizing question. Is American Judaism the disorganized remnant of a tradition once integrated, now in a shambles? Or do we discern something essentially different, newly emerging here in this land of freedom, the response of vital people to the challenges of modernity? I asked you to share your thoughts with me. The responses to that inquiry have been very heartening, as I sensed the readiness of the Congregation to confront the issues of Jewish life in our time.

The Congregation's Response

What impressed me deeply were the many and diverse expressions of concern about the character and possibilities of Jewish existence. Believing that answers exist, even though I do not know them all, I am greatly encouraged by the fact that so many of you, of varying backgrounds, ages and interests, are eager to share in the process of formulating those answers.

Jewish Collegians Reconsidered

We should moderate our newfound optimism with an awareness that some Jewish students are drifting and rootless. A student recently wrote me, "It seems clear to me that there are two basic trends manifesting themselves among American Jewish youth today. There are those who are falling away from any type of Jewish commitment. Conversely, there are those who are fiercely and sincerely dedicated to Judaism . . . I don't profess to know the answers to holding on to those marginal Jews, but I do know that we must go after them with the same proselyting vigor as do the Zen Buddhists and the Hare Krishnas and the various Christian sects to whom they are flocking in such numbers. These Jewish young people seek a faith that could be found in our own religion if they were not so ignorant of it."

Even though there is cause for concern, we can be uplifted by the sincerity and conviction of our Jewishly committed young people. The young Jew who knows a bit of Torah, who can understand the meaning of Hebrew songs and prayers, who knows what it means to talk tachlis, who knows that *Goodbye Columbus* is not the end-all of the Jewish experience and that aliyah is not the name of a new sports car, this young Jew may be a minority in modern day America, but he or she is a potent source of optimism. These young people are a cause for considerable gratitude, and they suggest to us, by their very presence, a new way of defining our relationship to America.

A New Contract

There is a rebellion among the young, which is not a rebellion against the past but a rebellion against the vacuous indifferentism into which they were reared. The vitality, the Jewish energy, that they exhibit suggest that we, as a group, should recapture our sense of Jewish authenticity. The time has come for us to renegotiate the terms of our contract with this country and, therefore, to redefine our understanding of ourselves. We know now at last how high the cost of the original contract has been. We might even raise the question as to whether America really expected accommodation as the price of freedom or whether the Jew had offered it out of gratitude for his new status as a citizen. Perhaps we had misunderstood America, and maybe America did not really want us to stop being Jews.

Furthermore, two hundred million people in this land will simply not be poured into a uniform mold. Black Americans, Chicanos, Indians, and ethnic groups are no longer prepared to sell their communal birthright. They seek an America as open to the group as America, up until now, has been open to the individual. So if we seek a new contract, it is with the belief that this day we are granted an opportunity that is rare and unique. The America of 1975 and beyond will not, I believe, be a reluctant party to this needed renegotiation. Today's America offers a new match between our needs and the possibilities of American culture.

Let us, however, make no mistake. We are not well prepared to take advantage of the opportunity. We have not even thought very much about it. It will not be easy. But if modesty is warranted, so also is a touch of chutzpah, because to put it bluntly, however inadequate or deficient we are, we can rely on no one else. The Jewish congregations assembled in this free land on Kol Nidre night comprise those human resources out of which Jewish life can be sustained and renewed. The well of nostalgia has dried up. Our pious ancestors have entered life eternal. There is no other Jewish community that has the opportunity for spiritual rebirth that has been conferred on us.

Guidelines for the Future

As we seek to articulate our task, define our program, and respond to this opportunity, I suggest three general guidelines for our renewal of purpose.

Acquiring a Jewish Lifestyle

One, we need to provide ways of acting Jewishly that are as varied, as ample, and as exciting as the modes of behavior that secular culture provides. We must rediscover our Jewish idiom and make that idiom a part of our lives and the lives of our children. We need to discover for ourselves how to find and create Jewish authenticity, Jewish Mentschlichkeit, Jewish family life. We know about Jewish public events: the establishment of the State of Israel, the Six-Day War, the October War, the struggle of Soviet Jewry. But our task is to recapture the memory of Jewish private events: what it means to be a Jewish person, to be a mentsch, to be part of a Jewish source of influence. The home is a primary Jewish experience, and that is where the future lies.

Chavurah

Chavurah refers to a small group of families usually, but not necessarily, with young children, who agree to meet regularly. They share, as Jews, in activities that express directly or indirectly, centrally or peripherally, their sense of Jewishness, their feeling of community. Interacting with each other as members of a Jewish fellowship, they visit each other's homes, they share each other's joys, they bring strength to each other in times of sorrow or difficulty.

Friday Evening in the Jewish Home

I address every Jewish woman with a plea to light the Sabbath candles and to kindle a special light of prayer and blessing in her home and in the hearts of her family.

I offer a similar plea to every Jewish man to make kiddush in the form and manner which allow him to express the sanctity of the Sabbath by his personal involvement.

We ask parents and children to do as much as you can—and then to do a little more. The Haggadah of Passover states that even if all of us are wise and even if all of us understand the Torah, it is our obligation to tell the story. In our circumstance, we have the right to reverse that dictum. Even though all of us are not all-wise, and do not know, and do not understand the entire Torah, it is still our mitzvah; it is still incumbent upon us to start learning and to begin to tell the story.

Federation and Synagogue

We need to redefine and restructure the agencies and institutions of our communal life. We must begin to remove the impenetrable wall that divides the synagogue community from Federation. We can no longer indulge in the luxury of maintaining barriers between the so-called secular and religious realms. The segregation of institutions and movements in Jewish life has always been a costly luxury, but ever since 1967, and particularly after 1973, this separation poses a danger to Jewish existence.

Those who are enlisted in the work of rescue and defense of the Jewish people are performing mitzvoth: the mitzvah of pikuach nefesh, "saving life"; the mitzvah of pidyon sh'vuyim, "ransoming captives"; the mitzvah of geulat haaretz, "redeeming the land." No Jew who is engaged in the struggle for Jewish survival should be labeled as a secularist, and many such Jews presently so labeled should consider the term offensive. Likewise the definition of "religious" in the formal sense alone is not valid. The synagogue Jew is not to be defined only in terms of his piety and observances, vital as they are, for he is also expected to commit himself to the worldly task of redemption, to the deliverance of Jews, and to the rebuilding of Eretz Yisrael. How encouraging it is to note that the Detroit Jewish community is moving forward toward these goals of greater Jewish unity and a deeper sense of shared purpose.

Persecution and Jewish Survival

A thoughtful congregant submitted to me a haunting, poignant comment: "I'm afraid that Judaism has survived mainly because in the final analysis, it was always forced, by outside pressures, to stand together or perish. So when the Jew believes he has attained almost equal status in the United States, and has lived to see the establishment of Israel, what unique drive does modern Judaism provide for him?"

I refuse to accept this widely held and rather pessimistic view of the Jewish future. I believe that it is possible to retain and nourish the Jewish spirit without continuing the Jewish tragedy. After the Holocaust, I would not offer anti-Semitism as the price for Jewish survival, for the price is simply too high.

I do not believe that God brought so many of our people to this blessed land in order to separate them permanently from His Torah. I do not believe that we American Jews were kept in life, preserved from the Holocaust, so that we might bow down to the gods of materialism or assimilation. A tradition which sustained so many generations of Jews under the most dreadful circumstances contains within itself enduring power, resilience, and rich promise.

Jews Are Different

That promise can be realized for us only if we admit to ourselves that we are different, that our differences from others matter, and that what is unique in our tradition is worth having. Our very existence as Jews gives us something precious to share with America. We need to commit ourselves radically and completely to our faith. And in order to do this, we must reconsider what it means to be a Jew. Implicit in what I have been saying is my conviction that being a Jew is both singular and excellent.

As representatives of the oldest unbroken tradition in the Western world, we Jews have a unique contribution to make to America—our hard-earned experiences in preserving those values which give meaning to human existence. As a community which has shared so largely in the benefits of American democracy, we have a responsibility to share those experiences. Our greatest contribution to America at this time in its history is to be Jewish.

Jewish Values and America's Crisis

In an article written several months ago, Eric Hoffer, an insightful observer of the contemporary scene, describes the dismay and vexation in our country. America wakes up one morning and finds itself "weirdly diminished and flawed. It finds its dollar devalued, its natural resources seriously depleted, its youth alienated, its armed forces demoralized, its manufacture shoddy, its workers negligent, its cities decayed and stewing in crime, its air and water polluted, and its leaders drained of confidence." Hoffer asks, "What are the essential attributes a country must have if it is to remain vigorous?" He replies, "Courage, a passion for excellence, hope and unbounded faith in the future."

Is it not our task to bring the truths of our own heritage to bear on

American culture today? We have a great deal to say about moral courage. The Jew remained constant in the face of unspeakable cruelty, refusing to be lured away from his ancestral faith either by the threat of force or the promise of reward. What other saga of moral courage could be more instructive and inspiring than the story that every Jew bears by his very existence?

A passion for excellence has been nurtured by the centuries in which the Jew had to struggle with adversity the way Jacob struggled with a dark angel. What is the passion for excellence if not a desire for learning, a concern for achievement, a zest for life, a commitment to the improvement of the world—all of which are so characteristic of the Jewish ethos? Should we not share that spirit with America by preserving the heritage which made us what we are?

To be a Jew means to affirm hope even though we could claim the luxury of self-pity or the questionable privilege of despair. Hope is woven into the very texture of Jewish worship, observance, and belief. We are people who accept death with the Kaddish, in which we look forward to the establishment of God's kingdom in the world. Should we not share with America our faith in the future, in the possibility of a world community sustained by brotherhood and peace? Our faith in man and his imperishable dreams should flow from our lives into the consciousness of our fellow citizens so that America's sense of national purpose can be reinvigorated and reaffirmed.

Thus, we are called upon to bear our uniqueness in this free and open society not as a burden, or as a wound, or as a hidden scar—not as something to be removed, cured, or forgotten—but as a powerful challenge, a high privilege.

Our Challenge

We should be prepared to pay the price, to run the risk, and hopefully and prayerfully to meet the crisis of freedom as effectively as we have met, in the past, the conditions of oppression and enslavement. The integration of Jews into America is about completed. We come today not as paupers or beggars into American society, bereft and forlorn, but as bearers of a rich heritage.

What we have given thus far to America has been through the medium of individuals—Hayim Solomon, Judah P. Benjamin, Louis D. Brandeis, Jonas Salk. In the next stage, we must make the Jewish people itself the source of blessing as a creative, vital society. Our task is to summon forth a vision of the future that can nourish our hope and fortify our will. That vision, inspired by the devotion of each generation that preceded us, will not only bring radiance to our lives but will also shed its light on our fellow Americans. As grave as is our crisis, so great is our opportunity, so rich the promise. If we meet the present challenge, we may bequeath to a coming generation a faith more mature and a community more secure than those which we inherited. Then will we be able to sing, "Am Yisrael Chai"—"The Jewish people lives." May coming generations add "Ad B'li Dai"—"So may it continue without end."

Keepers of the Dream

The topic I wish to explore emerged out of my experience with a group of young people during the course of this past year. Each year, I meet with the B'nai Mitzvah in addition to reviewing the Torah portion, and I take the time to know each child better. Sometimes we talk about school or sports or their hobbies or their plans for the next year. This year, I have been talking to each of our B'nai Mitzvah about their outlook on the world they inhabit. The question I ask is, "You are now thirteen, and this is the year 1976. In twenty-five more years, we will enter the year 2001, the beginning of the twenty-first century. The odds are in favor of your entering into that new millennium. Indeed, you have a better chance than your parents or grandparents to enter that new age. Tell me, do you think that the world will be better then than it is today? Will it be the same? Will it be worse?"

I have asked that question of between fifty and sixty children, and nine out of ten have said the world will be worse.

And when I asked them why, they gave me a number of reasons— they talked about pollution, the industrial threat to ecology, overpopulation, the danger of nuclear war, the depletion of our resources. What impressed me in these discussions was that evidently our young people do not expect the future to be better than the present. Indeed, they assume that the quality of life will deteriorate, that they have nothing to look forward to but the progressive decline in their physical and social environments.

What I find paradoxical is that these are the most affluent, the most privileged, and the best educated generation in human history, and yet they look upon the future with foreboding and apprehension. These young people are not prophets, and their predictions are not the product of scientific research. But what strikes me as sad and poignant is their bleak outlook, their pessimism.

I'm not sure how I felt when I was thirteen. We were in the middle of the Second World War. But I think that if I had been asked that question, I would have said I expected that in twenty-five years the world would be far better than it is today.

But these young people are expressing what they feel and sense are the prevailing attitudes of our time. They convey to us the message that we have communicated to them. A prevailing dismal view of the future—that famine, pollution, and expansion will bring about an inevitable collapse of the whole world order. According to a December 1975 Lou Harris poll, most Americans have accepted the thesis that the world is running out of food, energy, and other resources and that future economic growth must be limited. There is a new scientific specialty called futurology in which a whole new class of highly sophisticated doomsayers presents detailed analyses to prove that things could be worse and they soon will be. The essence of their conclusion is that the twenty-first century will see the greatest catastrophe since the Black Death of Europe in the Middle Ages. If this view seems exaggerated, consider the phenomenon that all movies—which are significant indicators of popular culture—which deal with the future portray a frightening world, a world without grass or trees or flowers, where people over thirty are not permitted to live and where violence has disrupted society so that totalitarian measures, including thought control and behavior manipulation, are universally practiced.

A recent cartoon in a national magazine, in an obvious reference to the biblical verse "The meek shall inherit the earth," shows a bearded gentleman walking through a garbage-infested and smoke-polluted street, carrying a sign which reads, "The meek don't want it."

What image of the future do we project for the Jewish community? Do we accept the verdict emanating from some quarters that there is no future Judaism in America; that it will undergo a slow, painless, but inevitable dissolution; that Jewish ignorance and assimilation and inter-marriage and attrition of loyalty will grow ever larger until they prove fatal? If we accept all this as the last word, as the vision of tomorrow, then of course all our synagogues and our religious schools and our camps Ramah and our Hillel day schools and our rabbinical seminaries and our Jewish homes are empty monuments to futility, and the better part of wisdom would be to give up, to throw in the tallith, and to announce to the world that the thirty-five-hundred-year-old drama has come to an end.

Project this view of tomorrow on the smaller screen of our personal lives. Each of us struggles with frustration, uncertainty, and all the con-tingencies of life. There are problems, challenges, disappointments to bring us concern and vexation. There are those perils which suddenly disrupt our lives: failing health, disabling illness, strife and discord within our families, the burden of bereavement, loneliness, confusion, turmoil. Is there any future, any tomorrow, any promise that we can look forward to?

Life without hope is an unending nightmare. If we could not hope for a second chance when life inflicts a severe defeat upon us, if we could not hope for strength when we have been betrayed, if we could not hope for healing when we have been bruised, if we could not hope for consolation when we have been bereaved—if in all these trials hope was denied us the burden of life would become insufferable.

How can we resist the counsels of despair and cynicism and discour-agement which may rob us of our most precious hopes and which have filled our children with pessimism and a sense of futility about their future? A brief episode, but it carries a profound significance. At the Academy Award presentations of this year, the distinction for the best supporting actress went to the remarkably talented Louise Fletcher, who played the role of the nurse in *One Flew over the Cuckoo's Nest.* When they called her to the stage to receive her Oscar, she said, "Thank you," over nationwide television in sign language to her parents, who are both deaf-mutes, "for teaching me how to hold on to a dream." What a remarkable statement. Parents who are deaf-mutes taught their child how to dream. Denied by cruel circumstance the capacity to hear and to speak, they had the ability to communicate to their child a dream that inspired, guided, and encouraged her to a career that brought fame and excellence.

The phrase has lingered in my mind. Judaism can be described in many ways, but it would not be inaccurate to characterize our religion as a heritage that teaches us how to hold on to a dream. We conclude every service with a dream that was originally part of the Rosh Hashanah liturgy. We repeat thrice daily, "Alkayn nekaveh L'cha"— "We therefore hope in Thee, oh Lord our God." We have a dream that there will be some day a world community living in brotherhood and in peace; we believe that there will be a day, a time, the messianic era, when man will have transcended the evils that lay life waste. We have a dream that though He tarries, the Messiah will come, and in that coming, and in hastening that coming, the Jew has had a role to play.

That dream, intensely and sacredly preserved, sustained Jewish life during centuries of persecution, degradation, and oppression.

There's a wonderful story about Rabbi Levy Yitzhak of Berdichev. The rebbe sent invitations to the wedding of his daughter with the announcement it would take place in Jerusalem in the court of the holy temple, with the Messiah and the high priest performing the ceremony. "If, however," the invitation continued, "the Messiah does not appear by that time, the wedding will take place next month in Berdichev."

Despite the horrors that have been endured by the Jewish generations of our time, despite the darkness of the Holocaust, despite the demonic forces that sought the destruction of our people, somehow the dream survives, the dream nourishes us, the dream keeps us alive.

To be a Jew means to be what Yehuda Halevi once called "a prisoner of hope." How else could we have survived in the face of all the evil designs that were cast against us? We are a people whose anthem is "Hatikva," which means "The Hope." We are a people who greet death with the Kaddish, in which we look forward to the establishment of God's kingdom of peace throughout the world.

And because we are "prisoners of hope," we do believe in the possibility of a world community living in brotherhood and in peace; we do believe in a Jewish community distinguished by a knowledge of its heritage, loyalty to its traditions, and commitment to its ideals. And because we are "prisoners of hope," we permit neither failure, nor perplexity, nor sorrow, nor even death to defeat us.

It has been said that hope without realism is an illusion. Realism without hope is despair. The integration of realism and hope builds endurance, devotion, and the capacity to act.

Are there other resources of hope that we can tap, besides the dream of the Messiah and the experiences of our ancestors? What other realities can sustain our hope?

A famous general was sitting in his tent one day during a crucial battle when a young lieutenant came rushing in with a map clutched in his trembling hands. "Look, General," he exclaimed, pointing to a position on the map, "the enemy is almost upon us."

"Young man," the general replied, "get larger maps. The enemy won't seem so close."

When the enemy of despair and discouragement closes in on us, we frequently need a larger map, a wider perspective of time and place. When we come to a point of crisis in life, it is easy to feel numb with the frightening thought that we are the first to confront this crisis. But as a matter of fact, each age has its own agonies, its own ordeals, its own tribulations.

The oldest piece of known writing in existence is found on a papyrus some six thousand years old, and it contains this complaint: "Alas, times are not what they used to be."

There is ample reason for concern about the moral, economic, and spiritual health of America, but I mention that in 1837, the *Detroit Free Press* wrote, "All is darkness and despair. As a nation, we are at the bottom of the hill."

In 1873, the *New York World* carried this somber estimate: "Collapse is a grim reality. The days of the republic are numbered."

And the *Wall Street Journal* in 1907 made the dreary proclamation: "The old ship of state is sinking. Even Morgan is using the subway."

We need larger maps. Herman Kahn, one of the prophets of doomsday, has recently issued a new perspective, one that expresses considerable confidence in mankind's ability to create a better future, and he believes the world's standard of living will continue to rise, economic growth will be possible, and increased knowledge and technology will successfully meet the challenges of the next century.

There is a second source for hope. It is found in the amazing resilience of the human being. I think often of that Yiddish expression which reminds us that the human being is weaker than a fly and stronger than iron. It is truly astonishing how much the human spirit can endure. There is a great deal of truth in the assurance of a wise man that God has given us no burden without the strength to carry it.

Some years ago, an elderly gentleman made the news in a rather unexpected way. He had been feeling pain around his abdomen and went to a doctor for a checkup. An X-ray examination revealed that there was a bullet comfortably lodged in his body. In response to this startling discovery, the patient recalled that he had been in some mishap thirty-seven years earlier. A gun was accidentally discharged, and he showed only a superficial wound. At the time, the doctor assured him that he had only been grazed by the bullet. After the surgery, he was shown the bullet, and the patient exclaimed half humorously, "I didn't know I had it in me."

Under much less dramatic circumstances, I have heard, as a rabbi, this statement repeated so many times. People who have gone through terrible sorrow, who have ministered to a loved one during an excruciatingly prolonged illness, who have withstood great stress and travail, as they look back upon the dreadful ordeal, frequently sigh in amazement, "I didn't know I had it in me."

There is an old French motto which reads, "Plus est en vous," which means "There is more in you." These words were carved above the gate of an old castle in France. The lords of the castle and its servants had the motto woven into its tapestries and banners and engraved upon their suits of armor. It is said to have inspired actions that made glorious history. There is indeed more in us than we commonly suspect. We have all kinds of unused stamina and courage and resilience and endurance which surface when life demands them of us. It is this human resiliency which fortifies our hope.

For the last, I have left a consideration of what is first—God as the source of hope.

In time of trouble and sorrow, people frequently ask, "Where is God? If there is a God, how could He permit this terrible thing to happen to me?" The prophets of Israel heard such questions from their people. Why did God permit us to be driven from our homeland, to taste defeat and homelessness, to endure exile and estrangement?

And the prophets of old gave a powerful answer to the question, Where is God? The answer—God is the power who will not let you succumb to despair. God is in your death-defying will to live. God is the strength which enables you to hope in the face of apparent hopelessness. God is the voice which urges you to hold on, to endure, to survive.

The God who spoke to our ancestors speaks to us.

When we are betrayed, He is our hope for vindication.

When we are bewildered, He is our hope for guidance.

When we are bruised, He is our hope for healing.

When we are bereaved, He is our hope for solace.

When we are confronted with the inescapable fact of our mortality, He is our hope for eternity.

To deny that there is a God is to deny that there is any ground for hope.

To deny that there is a God is to say that human beings must live and act without hope.

To deny that there is a God is to say that hope is the deceiver.

To deny that there is a God is to accept as the motto for human life that which Dante inscribed over the entrance to hell: "Abandon all hope, you who enter here."

In the great Judgment Day, one of the first questions we will be asked, according to our sages, is, Tsipeeta liyshuah?—Did you hope for redemption; did you keep the dream?

We cannot know what the year 5737 will be like, nor can we even attempt to discern what the world will be like in the year 2001. But we can, we must, renew in our hearts and transmit to our children the spirit of the psalm that we recite during this High Holiday season each morning and evening, the psalm that concludes with these words: "Hope in the Lord, be strong, let your heart take courage."

If we maintain our perspective, if we hold on to our faith in our own capacity, to our faith in God's power to see us through, then we can indeed hear the divine reassurance: "Blessed is the man that trusteth in the Lord, and whose hope the Lord is" (Jeremiah 17:7).

FORGIVENESS

Yom Kippur is not a day of penitence; it is the day of atonement. The penitent person is sorry for what he has done in the past; the atoned person is in the process of changing himself now.

—RABBI HENRY KAGAN

Forgive us, our Father, for we have sinned; Pardon us, our King, for we have transgressed.

—PRAYER

Guilt: Guardian of Our Goodness

This is the holiest night of the Jewish year, when we recite the familiar words of our confessional: "Oshamu"—"We have trespassed" and "Al Chet"—"for the sin we have sinned." Ten times during the atonement day service are these prayers repeated.

The main motif of the Yom Kippur ritual is its insistence on the deep sinfulness of human nature. Its first prayer, the celebrated Kol Nidre, is a formulation based on the premise that try as men will to do good, they must fail in some measure to live up to their commitments, wherefore each of them needs forgiveness.

Assembled in prayer, we rise, we beat the breast, we confess transgressions and iniquities.

Sometimes I wonder whether the neatly arranged prayers, the alphabetically organized confessions, and the acrostically composed meditations truly touch the hearts of modern Jews. I have the feeling that many worshipers do not sense they are being addressed by the service.

We recount our sins mechanically as they are listed in the liturgy. We read them like an airline schedule—and with as much enthusiasm. We recite them out of deference to the generations of our pious forebears. We dismiss them as relics of a premodern, unscientific era.

We are children of the Enlightenment, and we do not live in the same confined world as our ancestors, who perceived every rule as having issued from divine authority. We understand that conscience is nothing but the internalization of the moral standards that were inculcated in us in our childhood. We are aware that the superego is a product of conditioning. We recognize the phenomenon of guilt feelings, but we consider these to be the symptoms of troubled souls, personalities who have not resolved their inner conflicts or who have been subjected to unusual stress.

The feeling of guilt has had its legitimacy questioned in recent years. In the course of modern times, it has secured a bad name. It is to be viewed as the stuff other people lay on us. It has become known in the vernacular as a bad trip—one to be avoided at all costs. Those who provide us with such a burden are to be shunned, certainly ridiculed.

According to novelists and comedians, one of the heaviest traffickers in guilt is that much maligned character—the Jewish mother. All of the Jewish communal defense agencies—the Anti-Defamation League, the American Jewish Committee, the American Jewish Congress—have not been able to defend the Jewish mother, because her critics are generally Jewish. One stand-up Jewish comedian begins his routine with the one-liner "My mother is the East Coast distributor for guilt." A Jewish author and lecturer declares, "Guilt is to the Jews what oil is to Saudi Arabia, and we need an alternative form of energy."

Guilt is both mocked and trivialized. More people use the terms *guilt* and *sin* in relation to food than in reference to anything else. What is sin? A piece of cheesecake, a chocolate mousse, a gold brick sundae. A national advertisement for frozen fat-free yogurt made a theological statement: "All the pleasure. None of the guilt."

We are living in a guilt-free world. To be convinced of this assertion, it is necessary only to visit the local bookstore and consult the section on popular psychology. Purveyors of instant happiness have taken careful destructive aim at guilt. In a book entitled *Goodbye to Guilt*, the author, Gerald Jampolsky, contends that guilt pollutes and destroys a human being. I quote: "Guilt is the emotion we invented. It is both our jailer and the jail. It keeps our mind imprisoned and chained in the bondage of self-condemnation and depression."

Another author has a chapter on what he calls "the useless emotion—guilt and worry." He states that "complete freedom from guilt is one hallmark of healthy individuals—no lamenting the past, no effort to make others choose guilt by asking such inane questions as 'why didn't you do it differently?' or 'aren't you ashamed of yourself?' There are no standards to live up to but your own. Go ahead—give yourself permission."

How remarkable. Since the beginning of civilization, mankind has struggled over the issues of guilt and forgiveness, sin and atonement, but in the year 1990, we have solved these questions once and for all. There are no standards: "Give yourself permission."

Actually, this view is not as modern as it seems. It was the prevalent attitude in the decadent cultures of Babylon and Egypt and in the corrupt periods of Greek and Roman civilization. It explains the powerful, persistent appeal of paganism. Renounce morality, liberate yourself from ethical restraints, and indulge your desires.

The Bible is all about guilt—from the story of the first human beings through the history of Israel. The prophets of Israel offer one scathing condemnation after another of their people for oppressing the poor, for committing idolatry. The prophets threaten exile and destruction—tragedies that indeed did befall the people. Guilt was the message of Isaiah, Jeremiah, and Amos. What has now become of guilt? Have we completely removed its oppressive presence? No more guilt? Free at last?

In this enlightened time, we are drifting toward a no-fault morality, equivalent to no-fault insurance or no-fault divorce. No one else is to blame, as Dr. Karl Menninger once pointed out. When this or that awful thing is happening, and this terrible thing goes on, and that wretched circumstance develops, no one is responsible, no one is guilty, no moral questions are asked.

Why does the plague of violence continue to spread its ugliness over our major cities? Why are drugs ravaging the lives of millions, especially the young? Why are there no beds for the homeless or food for the hungry? Why is our environment being despoiled? Who is guilty?

The most compelling illustration is the savings and loan debacle, which will cost the American taxpayers over two hundred billion dollars in the years ahead. Who is responsible for this mismanagement of public funds, this betrayal of the public trust? Was it the officers of the banks? Was it our representatives, our senators? Was it the bank investors? Was it the government bank examiners? Was it the government? Who is guilty? Guilt cannot be assigned to anyone.

What happened to guilt? How were we able to rid ourselves of it so effectively and so thoroughly?

The answer is that our age has rejected the meaning of responsibility. The dictionary states that to be responsible means "to be answerable for the discharge of a duty, trust, or debt; to have the capacity to perceive distinctions of right and wrong; and it refers to accountability or obligation." Modern man is simply not accountable. He is not accountable to God; his community; his employer; his parents, spouse, or children. He is not accountable to past generations, whose labor and sacrifice have made his privileges possible. He is not accountable to the generations of the future, whose destiny is affected by his life.

Modern man is in flight from responsibility. The prophet who belongs most closely in temperament to our age is Jonah, whose words constitute the Haftarah.

The story begins with the word of God coming to Jonah to tell him to arise and go to Nineveh, a great city, and cry against it, for their wickedness has come "up before me"—truly a reasonable request to ask of any of God's prophets. But Jonah's reaction was peculiar. He runs away. He gets down to a handy seaport and hops a boat to Spain, which is in the opposite direction.

Why did Jonah run away? Was it because he was afraid? After all, if the word of God came to a person of this generation to arise and go to Baghdad and cry against it because of its wickedness, he or she might think twice about it and take a cruise to the Hawaiian Islands. But Jonah was no coward.

The reason Jonah ran away was because Jonah was uncertain—not of what might happen to him but of what might happen to the people of

Nineveh. They might repent, and then God, instead of punishing them, would forgive them. So he would be embarrassed and humiliated because his prediction had not come to pass. Why should he get involved with them? He didn't want to be responsible for them. So he thought he could run away from his duty as spokesman of God's truth.

The flight from responsibility is as old as the opening verses of the Book of Genesis. It is as old as man himself. Adam, in a garden, eats from the forbidden tree. God confronts him with the accusing question, "Hast thou eaten of the tree whereof I commanded thee, that thou shouldest not eat?"

What does Adam answer? Adam takes it like a man. He blames his wife. "Woman, whom thou gavest to be with me, she gave me of the tree and I did eat." It was her idea, not mine.

But women need not feel superior, I point out that evading moral responsibility is not exclusively a masculine affliction. In the same biblical incident, God turns to Eve and says, "What is it that thou has done?" Eve is ready. She says, "The serpent beguiled me and I did eat." The serpent, not being human, remains silent and doesn't blame anyone.

Judaism has an important message for us. The conscience is real, and a guilty conscience can be useful. I recognize the phenomenon of neurotic guilt, the fact that some lives are disturbed by fits of depression and moods of melancholy or consumed by remorse for sins and transgressions that are more imaginary than real. One may encounter individuals who suffer grievously from a sense of guilt that is unfounded and unjustified. They believe they have not lived up to impossible standards which they have set for themselves.

I think of a man, a Holocaust survivor, who for years lived with the guilt that he could not save his wife and his parents from the destruction that came upon his family. That he did not contribute to their deaths did not diminish his self-accusation until many years passed.

I think of the guilt that consumes parents when their children don't turn out the way they had hoped. They ask the unanswerable question, What did I do wrong? As though any parent is omnipotent and has total control in determining the course of a child's life.

But there is real guilt, and there is a difference between real guilt that arises out of a bad moral choice and neurotic guilt. Our Kol Nidre service, and the whole outlook of Judaism, asserts that we are responsible. We err; we fail; we fall short of our ideals; and we are, therefore, guilty. When I discussed this with a friend and colleague, he said, "If I were ever to make a mistake, I would admit it."

Paradoxically, the recognition of guilt is a measure of respect for human capacity, for the human potential. It says that every individual is capable of more than he has yet done. We have misused psychiatry, or a distorted form of psychiatry, to evade self-confrontation, to deny human freedom. Listen to Anna Russell and her psychiatric folk song: "At three, I had a feeling of ambivalence toward my brothers, and so it follows naturally, I poisoned all my lovers. But now, I am happy; I have learned a lesson this has taught; that everything I do that's wrong is someone else's fault."

When we rise for the confessional, we say, "Chatati"—"I have sinned." All of us want to avoid guilt. We would rather blame heredity, circumstance, God, anybody. In the noteworthy play by Archibald MacLeish, *J.B.*, three comforters come to a modern Job. One is a Christian who says, "It's not your fault; you are the victim of unconscious drives you can't control." Then Job says, "No, I want to be responsible. I want it to be my fault, because that is what it means to be a human being. It means to say, 'I have the power to choose the moral content of my life.'"

What the Jewish tradition proclaims is that whether we like it or not, we are accountable, individually and collectively. Responsibility is more than duty, something imposed upon us from the outside. In its truest sense, it is a voluntary act. It is my response to the need of another human being and to my highest conception of myself. Because I am human, I cannot evade involvement in the world around me. I am a husband, a father, a brother, a Jew, a rabbi, a citizen. I am related to other people; my life is joined to theirs. I feel accountability to the persons, to the group, to the institutions, through whom and by whom I define myself.

Responsibility reaches its peak when it thrusts me outward to concern and love. If husband and wife love each other, they will welcome the fullest possible kind of responsibility for each other. If a person loves his country, no sacrifice will be too great on its behalf. If we love our people, we are prepared to bear its burdens as well as participate in its joys. If we love our heritage, we will be loyal to its ideals and values. If we love God, we will be responsible for serving as His partner in Tikkun Olam, in improving the world which He created.

The time has come for us to take a new look at the Jewish mother stereotype. As Francine Klagsbrun wrote a few months ago, "God knows, we don't seem to have improved much as parents since we began renouncing the Jewish mother way. Our adolescent suicide has doubled in the last two decades, drug abuse continues to plague many families, and cults lure the innocent and insecure."

What of those demands and expectations Jewish-mother types have placed on their children? Sure, when parental demands exceed the abilities of a child, they can be dangerous and destructive. But we've also seen the dangers of leaning over backward not to pressure kids, not to burden them with expectations. The results are young people who feel confused, lacking in self-discipline, reluctant to put themselves on the line. Intelligent "pushiness" often pushes children to stretch as far as they can.

And what about guilt? There is guilt and there is guilt. A mother threatens to put her head in the stove at the slightest sign of disobedience; that's a bad use of guilt. But parents have to set standards. If you forbid your fifteen-year-old son to drink beer at a party and he drinks anyway, his feeling guilty may prevent his drinking next time—or the time after that. This is guilt well used. Jewish mothers of old knew this. They stood firm on what they believed to be right or wrong and minced no words in conveying those beliefs. Many of us today have lost either our convictions or our ability to transmit them, or both, and many "guilt-free" kids are the worse for it. To Jewish mothers, I say, "Come out; we need you now. We want to observe you. We want to learn from you. And we want to celebrate with you with the traditional toast of our people: L'Chayim, may you live and be well, and go on mothering for one hundred and twenty years." *Yasher Koach* to Francine Klagsbrun.

Of course, there is something in us that would prompt us to shun obligations and evade being held accountable. I remind you of the cartoon by Jules Pfeiffer in which he depicts a person hiding his head under a blanket. The individual says, "When I was five, they made me go to school, and I wasn't ready. When I was ten, they made me go to camp, and I wasn't ready. When I was eighteen, they made me go to the army, and I wasn't ready. When I was twenty-one, they made me get married, and I wasn't ready. And now that I am fifty, I am going to stay in here and I'm not coming out, and I'm not going to grow up until I am ready." The cartoon has won fame because a part of us does not want to grow up, does not want to assume responsibility. There is a child within us that chafes at the rules, that cannot see beyond the gratification of the moment. But a child cannot understand and does not sin. We understand, and we transgress.

We are all tempted, like Jonah, to escape the realities of life, to avoid responsibility. We cannot do this without destroying the only meaning and dignity that human existence possesses.

A husband and a wife came to see me some time ago. The man had done something very reprehensible to his wife, which affected the stability of their marriage. And I said to the man, "Is it true? Did you really do this?" And his answer was, "It is not my fault. She got me mad, and you can't hold me responsible for what I did when I was upset."

Two teenagers came to see the rabbi together with their parents. They had gotten in trouble with the law. And when he asked them, "Why did you do it?" their answer was, "It wasn't our fault. We were out with our friends, and they dared us to do it, so we had to."

A couple came to see a counselor. They were involved in an incredibly complicated tangle of legal and moral confusions. And the counselor asked the woman, "How could you possibly get into this situation?" And her answer was, "It wasn't our fault. We got carried away by emotion, and there was nothing we could do."

The issue is not what they did but their failure to accept responsibility for what they did.

Deep down in our hearts, we know when we have strayed. We are annoyed with ourselves. We are aware of the deficiencies, the pettiness, the duplicities, the infidelities, the needless injuries, and all the other sordid episodes of our lives. We all fail now and then. Husbands fail; wives fail; parents fail; children fail. We are not always faithful to family and friends. We have not always adhered to the highest demands of our heritage as Jews, and we excuse ourselves. We have various forms of evasion. We find someone or something to serve as our whipping boy, to carry the burden of responsibility and guilt we are unwilling to assume.

We are reminded of the cartoon of a little boy who is looking at a report card in which the young student has a failing grade in each of his courses. The father scowls. The son says, "What do you think it is, Dad, heredity or environment?"

Every alleged mistake on our part has to be explained as someone else's fault. It reminds me of a bumper sticker I saw: "The man who can smile when things are going badly has just thought of someone to blame it on."

Nietzsche once wrote, "An uneasy conscience is a sickness. But it is a sickness akin to pregnancy." In other words, it bears within itself the seed of a new life.

What is the value of a guilty conscience? Guilt reminds us of our responsibilities. It recalls to us our commitments. When we face our guilt, we simultaneously draw a measure of respect for human capacity, for human potential.

Yom Kippur challenges me to confront my guilt: to confess it, to face it, and to transform it into a power for growth, for good. Not everything that is faced can be changed, but nothing can be changed until it is faced. We can change ourselves; we can change our community.

I do not know how to define the Jew but in the terms we have been using—an involved, concerned, and accountable person. I do not know how to explain either Jewish history or Jewish faith but as the expression of an almost boundless sense of responsibility. The Jew is characterized as Zocher Ha-brith, one who kept faith with the Covenant. He was accountable to his community, his God, his people, and future generations. This is the key to our existence, and with it, we open the doors to the choicest treasures of Jewish experience and moral achievement.

We should return to these treasures. We should reaffirm on this day of atonement these great principles not only for the purpose of self-discipline but also in order to release the best that is within us.

To believe in the power of Teshuvah, or repentance, means to have a very high estimate of who we are. We are not asked to grovel before our Maker in self-abasement but rather to rise to a high sense of self-esteem. We are greater than we realize. We have the power to conquer the selfishness which diminishes us, the lust which enslaves us, the callousness which binds us.

A leading psychiatrist once wrote, "If the concept of personal responsibility and answerability for ourselves and for others were to return to common acceptance, hope would return to the world with it."

We, as Jews, carry the seeds of that hope. As Jews, we taught the world that the measure of a person is taken in how much he cares and about how many he cares. This is the burden of being human. This is the glory of being human. May God grant us the insight to understand our responsibilities and the courage to fulfill them with love and faith. Thus shall we attain the grandeur of the human spirit that is the vision of this sacred day. Thus shall we merit the fulfillment of the divine promise: "Salachti, Kidvorecha"—"I have forgiven Thee, according to Thy word."

The Sin of Words

What is Kol Nidre?

At first glance, it is a technical formula to annul vows. But at the root of it, one finds the distinctive Jewish conviction that a word is sacred and cannot therefore be treated cavalierly.

Kol Nidre is about words. Words and promises we didn't keep. Words and dreams we wish we had kept. The words we said and wish we hadn't. The words we didn't say and wish we had.

The power of words is awesome, our words and the words of others which we read and hear. Words can be a curse, and they can be a blessing. In our tradition, God is portrayed as having created the world through the instrumentality of words—ten utterances.

And God said, "Let there be light."

Folk culture says that words are cheap. Words are not cheap, says Kol Nidre, they are immeasurably holy. Consider the Al Chet, the confessional. What prominence is given to the sanctity of the words "For the sin which we have committed before Thee with utterance of the lips; by impure speech; by denying and lying; by scoffing; by slander; by idle gossip; by tale bearing; by swearing falsely . . . and more."

The entire confessional is followed by the silent devotion which we repeat thrice daily—"Oh my God, guard my tongue from evil and my lips from speaking deceit."

We are warned against the vulgarization of language. A story is told of a man who boarded a train in New York late one evening. He gave the porter five dollars to make sure that he got him up early in the morning to get off at Syracuse, where he had an important meeting. When he awakened, he discovered that the sun was shining. He rang for the porter and asked where they were. "We'll be getting into Buffalo in a short time," said the porter, whereupon the traveler burst into a tirade of unmentionable expletives, terrible language. The Pullman conductor overheard the scene and called the porter aside. "Look, you are expected to be courteous, but you don't have to stand talk of that kind." "Oh," said the porter, "if you think that was bad, you should have heard the man I put off at Syracuse."

It's not only lapsing into profanity. It is the whole tenor of crudity, vulgarity, and meanness which is becoming the vogue.

The mahzor reminds us of the sin of L'shon Hara, wickedness, evil speech, slander. I saw a cartoon of two women who were preparing to board an airliner. One of them turns to the pilot and says, "Please don't travel faster than sound; we want to talk." Talk is enjoyable. The juicier it is, the more enjoyable. We all understand that you can't believe everything you hear, but you can repeat it. I like that definition which describes a gossip as a person who will never tell a lie when the truth will do as much damage.

L'shon Hara is the tongue of wickedness. It is rated as a cardinal sin. The Talmud declares, "Whoever engages in gossip, it is as if he or she denies the very essence of faith." Evil speech is more destructive than murder, say the sages in the midrash, for a murderer kills but one individual, whereas he who indulges in gossip kills three—the speaker, the spoken to, and the spoken of.

Our entire society encourages gossip. We recognize the accepted institution of the gossip columnist. Here is a professional whose business, quite literally, is to write about what is none of his or her business.

When we aren't careful in the way we bandy about words, when we misuse language, we are apt to bring a desanctification of man himself.

A father lectures his son.

"I never told lies when I was your age." The boy allowed a moment to pass and then with curiosity asked, "How old were you when you started, Dad?"

Is there any unnecessary cruelty in the world? It is certainly the cruelty to which we are all addicted in one form or another with hardly an exception—the cruelty of the evil tongue. Here we are, all of us, enduring frustration and pain and the ravages of time, all of us engaged in the difficult task of meeting life's obligations and coping with its stresses. One would imagine that we would have some sympathy for our fellow human beings, who, like us, must carry their burdens along life's journey. But this is not our practice. We make life a little more difficult, a little more unpleasant, for our fellows, although this is neither required or necessary or advantageous.

Am I referring to lying? Not exactly. The sages say that even telling the truth with malicious purpose is L'shon Hara if it is intended to bring pain and anguish to another.

L'shon Hara is that special pleasure that we discover in talking about our neighbor's weakness, the secret delight we find in disclosing his sins.

The terrible thing about the malicious word is that it is so irretrievable. An old Jewish story tells of a woman who came to her rabbi on a wintry day with a terrible sense of guilt. She had spread a very unkind story about another woman in the town and had just learned that the story had no basis whatever in fact. What should she do?

The rabbi told her that she would have to do two things. First, she would have to take the feathers from one of her pillows and place one feather on the doorstep of each of the houses in the little town. After she completed this task, she should return, and the rabbi would give her a second task. The woman left and returned the following day. "What shall I do now?" she asked. "Now," said the rabbi, "go gather up all the feathers from each of the houses where you put them."

"But, Rabbi," protested the woman, "that is impossible. The wind has already scattered them far and wide." "Indeed, it has," said the rabbi. "To gather up those feathers is as impossible as to take back the harsh words you spoke. You would do well to remember that before you speak in the future."

What about words uttered in anger? How many families have they divided? How many friendships have they fractured? How many marriages have they injured? How many yet unhealed wounds have they caused?

Once evil words have been spoken, they take on lives of their own and leave damage and destruction in their path. Therapists' offices are filled with people who are in anguish about words spoken to them or about them. Sometimes the words float in conscious memory, heard over and over again as a drumbeat of anguish. Sometimes they rest just below the surface, resurrected now and then to mock and to taunt.

Slander and gossip are not victimless crimes. Words do not just dissipate into thin air. They come home to roost, to affront and harass.

Scripture declares, "Life and death turn on the power of the tongue."

One might argue that there are greater problems that confront us today, issues that agitate our country and our society. Perhaps the larger issues that confront us are the working out of the smaller evils that often elude our attention and our grasp.

In the crime of gossip or slander, it is very hard to find the culprit, and the victim doesn't have to be present. The injury is other than theft and is far more destructive. I quote Shakespeare: "Good name in man and woman, dear my lord, / Is the immediate jewel of their souls: / Who steals my purse steals trash; 'tis something, nothing; / 'Twas mine, 'tis his, and has been slave to thousands; / But he that filches from me my good name / Robs me of that which not enriches him, / And makes me poor indeed."

A cocktail party has been defined as a place where they cut sandwiches and friends into little pieces. The French philosopher Pascal declared that if all men knew what each said of the other there would not be four friends in the world. And long before Pascal, the prophet Zechariah complained, "I was wounded in the house of my friend."

Of course we don't gossip. We engage in what a friend of mine calls "character analysis." But if we want to know how to define the so-called character analysis, we should ask ourselves these questions. How would you feel if it were said about you? How would you feel if it were communicated to the person involved? Would you be willing to say it directly? Is it true? Is it fair? Is it necessary?

The Jewish tradition has been deeply intent upon defining the characteristics of L'shon Hara. It deems this one of the most important moral issues and is outraged when it takes place on high levels. Why is this?

I believe it is because of the experiences of the Jewish people themselves. We have been accused as Jews of every sin, of every vice, of every form of depravity. In the Middle Ages, when the crops didn't grow and the rain didn't fall and the dread plague struck, the medieval mind saw this as the product of the evil power of Jews who lived in their communities. Enemies of the Jews have characterized us as vagabonds, cosmopolitans, and parasites. The Nazis called us Communists, and the Communists called us Nazis. Even today, there are anti-Semitic journals that circulate the most absurd lies, fabrications about the Jewish people. There is such a thing as collective slander. There is a form of gossip which is not only destructive to an individual but can make a total people an object of hatred, derision, and contempt.

Paul Johnson, in his *History of the Jews*, wrote, "One of the principal lessons in Jewish history has been that repeated verbal slanders are sooner or later followed by violent physical deeds. Time and again over the centuries, anti-Semitic writings created their own fearful momentum, which climaxed in an effusion of Jewish blood."

We Jews are especially sensitive to the high cost of slander because rivers of Jewish blood have been shed because of the wicked myths and calumnies that have been spread about us. For every word in *Mein Kampf*, a hundred and twenty lives were to be lost. For every page, forty-seven hundred lives. For every chapter, more than one million two hundred lives. The price of such evil language is monstrously exorbitant.

Maybe that is why we were so sensitive about anti-Semitic language

when Michael Jackson made a new album on which he used an exple-
tive that rhymes with "bike" (I will omit the word) and the phrase "sue
me, Jew me." We knew that millions of people around the world would
be hearing these ugly words, and we are aware of what has happened to
us before when nasty words were spoken about us. It was Steven Spielberg who had the most influence in getting Jackson to change the
objectionable words, because Spielberg had just finished *Schindler's
List* and the cost that words could exact in human casualties was fresh
in his mind. And Michael Jackson changed the album and the song. A
journalist wrote in response, "Watch your thoughts. They become
words. Watch your words; they become actions. Watch your actions;
they become habits. Watch your habits; they become character. Watch
your character; it becomes your destiny."

It has not been my practice to speak about political matters or to
express opinions about political campaigns. But I speak now not in a
partisan way but rather from the perspective of the moral values of the
Jewish tradition. As the presidential campaign of '96 gets under way
this year, we will all be subject to the impact of campaign rhetoric. The
last several presidential campaigns have become more and more ugly.
Seemingly, the words acquire deeper levels of viciousness. The worse
you can smear your opponent, the better your changes of winning.

A lawyer told me once that in his first year of law school, an experienced attorney told him, "When you have the facts, you pound the
facts; when you have the law, you pound the law; when you have neither, you pound the table." We observed this in the scenes of the O. J.
Simpson trial.

Sometimes one senses our political campaigns are exercises in
pounding the table. For those who have no real issues, no visions, no
solutions, all that is left is either to shout ugly words or pound the table
and make a lot of noise.

I apply our thought to the Oklahoma City bombing. After that catastrophic tragedy, President Clinton gave an important speech in which
he blamed the mass destruction of life partly on the rhetoric of violence
in our society, in our world. "We hear so many loud and angry voices

today . . . They spread hate . . . Bitter words can have consequences . . .
They leave the impression that violence is acceptable. When they talk
of violence, we must stand up against them."

It didn't help. The next day the talk on the airwaves was about him
and how dare he tell us how to behave. The call-in talk shows that week
revealed so much anger, so much ridicule.

Anthony Lewis made an excellent point after the Oklahoma City
bombing when he said that certain fanatic segments of American society have so demonized their opponents as un-American, treasonous,
peculiar that it isn't any wonder that violence ensues. The drumbeat of
extremist rhetoric in the last few years has seen Washington as the
enemy, the inhuman monster. Has that no connection with the rise of
groups that claim federal agents are about to descend on them in black
helicopters? Words matter.

The particular ideology that takes credit for these murders is a mix-
ture of white supremacy, antigovernment nativism, and anti-Semitism.
Oklahoma City was a wake-up call to this country. Wake up to the danger of words: the military training manuals; the anti-American tracts;
the computer programs which teach how to build bombs and wage wars
of terrorism against democracy; and the propaganda tracts, which contain rewritten Nazi materials. The message of Oklahoma City to America is "Lower the rhetoric; control your rage; speak carefully and mind-
fully. Beware of extremism."

The debasement of language and its mean-spirited use are everywhere. A prominent actress and comedienne, who revels in vulgarity,
cohosted a video awards program. Her opening remarks were "I'm not
upset about my divorce. I'm only upset that I am not a widow." Is that
entertainment?

In sports, on the basketball court, it's not enough to dunk the ball. It
has to be followed by "talking trash" to your opponents. In football, no
player seems to be able to carry the ball for a touchdown without following it up with a taunting dance. Whatever happened to sportsman-
ship?

I think of what has happened to the Jewish people as a consequence of the peace process. Passions are running very high in Israel and in American Jewry. The right wing believes that territorial concessions will jeopardize Israel's security. The Labor government believes that signing a peace treaty with the Palestinians is the best method of creating long-term security for the State of Israel. Language becomes a weapon, and each side accuses the other of undermining the foundations of the state and betraying the trust of the Jewish people.

One painful example of the level of discourse involves General Danny Rothschild of Israel. He is a dove. It is his right. He may be right; he may be wrong. However, he came to New York City this year, to Queens, to speak in favor of the peace process. A heckler got up and insulted him, called him a traitor, and accused him of endangering Israel's security. The annoying heckler went further to say, "Coward! How dare you give up the Golan? Was it because you are afraid to fight for it?" Rothschild looked at him and said, "No, it is because I already left one limb on the Golan, fighting to get it."

We must never forget that we are all brothers, we are all Jews, and we share a common fate.

On Thursday, in Washington, DC, the prime minister of Israel, Yitzhak Rabin, and the leader of the PLO, Yasser Arafat, signed a complex document which provides for interim transfer of autonomy to a number of areas on the West Bank to the Palestinian authority. The government of Israel has pursued the policy of the peace process with difficulty. The partner, that is to say, Yasser Arafat and the PLO, is deeply disliked. The partner has not faced Hamas and prevented terrorist actions, which have continued during all these months. Is the PLO committed to peace and dependable enough? Is the proposed peace worth the price in lost territory and in historical memory and in weakened national unity? Is Israel undermining its security? These are legitimate and difficult questions. But what has happened is that the opposition has voiced its disapproval of any territorial concessions. Spokesmen have poured their vituperation on the government and used terms like *traitor* and *criminal* about the prime minister.

And the government has overreacted to peaceful protest. The social fabric of the people of Israel is being pulled apart. There must be civility in the discourse on the issues. Israel is engaged in a hazardous search for a true and lasting peace. The Rabin government seeks to end once and for all the bloody Palestinian-Israeli confrontation. The government is willing to take risks. Are we apprehensive? Of course. Are we fearful of terrorist outrages? Surely. Are we uncertain of the future? Without doubt. But not withstanding our deep distrust of the PLO and its leaders, I believe the majority of American Jews support the search for peace.

Finally, we don't live in Israel. Our children and grandchildren do not serve in the Defense Forces of Israel. We have not earned the right to dissent from Israel's government on issues vital to her security. We need to pray for each other—with each other—to pray for peace, and for wisdom and understanding, and for Ahavat Yisrael.

There is a wonderful Jewish expression whose deeper meaning I did not grasp until now: "Ha Chayim Vihammavet Biyad Ha-Lashon"— "Life and death are in the power of the tongue." The tongue can heal and give hope; the tongue can crush and bring death.

Yom Kippur confronts us with the sins of speech—words we say that we should not say.

Someone has written that "kind words are the music of the world. They have a power which seems to be beyond natural causes . . . It seems as if they could almost do what in reality God alone can do." Everyone feels grateful at one time or another. It's just that a word of thanks doesn't strike us as being overly important, so we don't get around to expressing it.

It has been said that no matter how flat your conversation, most people would like to have it flatter. Sometimes what we really deserve is not flattery but a compliment. But is it so important to tell her in so many words that she did well? Maybe not to you, but to her, very important. A contemporary author writes, "Speech may sometimes do harm, but so may silence, and worse harm at that. No offered insult ever caused so deep a wound as a tenderness expected and withheld."

Words we should say but don't say—like words of thanks and admiration and love and encouragement.

There are some husbands and wives who wait to hear a word of love from each other but it never comes. They take each other for granted, assume that their love for each other goes without saying, and therefore, neither ever tells the other that what each of them longs to hear. There are some parents who love their children deeply and yet cannot get themselves to utter the words their children want so desperately to hear. A man once told me that his father has been dead for many years. And he keeps on having the same recurring dream: His father comes to visit him and says, "I forget to tell you, son, I love you very much." Some of us are still waiting to hear (or to say) those words, even long after our parents are gone.

The prophet Hosea had all this in mind when he said, "Take words with you and return to the Lord."

A commentator made this observation. "God says, 'I do not ask of you silver or gold when you come to repent. All I ask of you is words, but let them be good words.'"

What beautiful words we shall speak during these next twenty-four hours. We shall give expression to remorse; we shall frame great resolves; we shall echo the undying hopes of the Household of Israel. Each of us is given the power to bless the people in our lives with words of cheer, words of warmth, words of support, healing and soothing words.

Words can soften grief, can lift our sagging spirit. Kind words are the passkey to every heart. Three times each day, at the end of the silent devotion, we pray to God, "May the words of my mouth and the meditation of my heart find favor before You, my rock and my redeemer."

Forgiveness

What is the goal of Yom Kippur? The most obvious answer is for us to be reconciled with God. Thus, the purpose of Yom Kippur is to face our transgressions; to confront our sins; to focus on our shortcomings; and to resolve to do Teshuvah, to repent.

Of course, Yom Kippur inspires us to address these fundamental issues. But, I believe, the most urgent and compelling message of this day is expressed in a different theme, a theme which we do not consider often enough, which is why we need a holiday dedicated to it. The goal is forgiveness, or Mechilah. Yom Kippur calls upon us to exercise this demanding and heroic act.

Each catalog of sins, each series of transgressions, each formulation of the confessional is followed by the words *Selach Lanu, Mechal Lanu, Kaper Lanu* (Forgive us, pardon us, grant us atonement).

From the opening lines of Kol Nidre and the verses which follow it, this whole day is about forgiving and being forgiven. Why this constant emphasis?

The answer lies within our hearts.

During the course of a year, many of us have permitted our lives to become constricted by feuds, grudges, resentments. Some of us made decisions years ago that we weren't going to speak to someone anymore or let him into our lives, decisions we have kept more faithfully than most promises made to ourselves.

A story is told of a man who had too much to drink at a party, made a foolish spectacle of himself, and then passed out. Later, he was very remorseful, and he asked his wife to forgive him. She said she understood and that she would forgive and forget. However, as the months went by, she would refer to the incident from time to time. After awhile, he became tired of hearing about it. "I thought you said you were going to forgive and forget," he said. "I have forgiven and I have forgotten," she said, "but I just don't want you to forget that I have forgiven and forgotten."

Once we have acted wrongly, or once others have acted wrongly toward us, no one simply forgets the unpleasant experience.

During this season, and particularly on this day of Yom Kippur, we seek forgiveness for our own misdeeds from God, but we cannot solicit forgiveness unless we practice it. We cannot even believe that God forgives unless we can feel the power to do the same. We cannot merit God's forgiveness for ourselves unless we are capable of extending it to others. The ancient rabbi Ben Sira taught, "Forgive your neighbor and then, when you pray, your sins will be forgiven."

There are many husbands and wives whose love for one another once filled their souls with beauty but who now experience lives of estrangement and emotional distance, although they live under one roof.

Why is this?

Because marriages tend to be founded on romantic love. We feel swept away by feelings of rapture, but the essence of marital love is not romance but forgiveness.

Forgiveness, as the truest form of love, means accepting without bitterness the flaws and imperfections of our partner and praying that our partner accepts our flaws as well. Romantic love overlooks faults. Mature marital love sees faults clearly and forgives them, understanding that there are no perfect people, that we don't have to pretend perfection, and that an imperfect spouse is all that an imperfect person like us could aspire to. I remember a lady who told me, "For years, I was looking for the perfect man, and when I finally found him, it turned out he was looking for the perfect woman, and that wasn't me."

There are many parents and children who barely talk to each other, who ceased communicating with one another long ago. Their harsh judgments about each other conceal and suppress the love that lies deep beneath the surface.

Belonging to the same family does not protect us from being hurt by, jealous of, and even hating our relatives.

Anyone who doubts it has only to take an inventory of his own family. Almost certainly, there is at least one branch of it he has never met or at least has not spoken to in many years. It's Aunt Tillie, who won't sit at the same table as Aunt Martha, or Cousin Mervin who refuses to come at all because Uncle Sam will be there.

We seem to have a need for a "hate parade" in our lives—the former partner who cheated us, the employer who let us go without cause, the spouse who left us for another. We cling to our anger. We become attached to our resentments, we nurse and nurture them, and we will not let them go.

How can we forgive those who have committed offenses against us, who insulted us, who hurt us, who wronged us in some way, whom we swore we would never talk to again, who never asked our forgiveness, who perhaps never acknowledged their doing anything wrong? How do we rid ourselves of those grudges which are eating away at our kishkes and stop seeking revenge? How do we forgive and yet deal with the reality that we will never really forget what others did to us?

Some time ago, I came upon a cartoon of an elephant lying on a psychiatrist's couch, dabbing his eyes with a tissue. The psychiatrist is telling him, "Of course, I know you will never forget, but you need to work on forgiving." We are the elephant. We will never forget, but we too need to work on forgiving.

A man complained to his friend that whenever his wife gets angry, she becomes historical. "You mean hysterical," the friend corrected him. "No," said the husband, "I mean historical. She starts listing everything I did wrong in the last twenty-seven years." Beware of that sentence erupting in the middle of an argument that begins with "You always . . ." or "You never . . ."

The embarrassing secret is that many of us are reluctant to forgive. We nurture grievances because that makes us feel morally superior. Withholding forgiveness gives us a sense of power, often power over someone who otherwise leaves us feeling powerless. The only power we have over them is the power to remain angry at them. At some level, we enjoy the role of being the long-suffering, aggrieved party. The Talmud discusses this issue and says that the normal life span of a quarrel is two or three days. If a person hurts or offends you, you are entitled to be upset with him for that long. If the bitter feelings extend into a fourth day, it is because you are choosing to hold on to them; you are nursing the grievance, keeping it on artificial life support, instead of letting it die a natural death.

There may be a certain emotional satisfaction in claiming the role of victim, but it is a bad idea. This estranges you from the person you could be close to. Even more, it accustoms you to seeing yourself in the role of victim—helpless, passive, and preyed upon by others. Holding grudges deprives us of our freedom; it limits us, controls us, contorts our lives.

I recall counseling a divorced woman who was seething about her husband's having left her for another woman years ago and having fallen behind on child support payments. She would ask me, "How can you expect me to forgive him after what he has done to me and the children?" My answer was, "I'm not asking you to forgive him because what he did wasn't so terrible. It was terrible. I suggest that you forgive him because he doesn't deserve to have this power to turn you into a bitter, resentful woman. When he left, he gave up the right to inhabit your life and mind to the degree that you are letting him. Your being angry at him doesn't harm him, but it hurts you. It is turning you into someone you don't really want to be. Release that anger, not for his sake—he probably doesn't deserve it—but for your sake, so that the real you can reemerge."

Rabbi Harold Kushner writes about a columnist for a Boston paper who tells this story. She remembers sitting in a park watching children at play. Two children got into an argument and one says to the other, "I hate you. I am never going to play with you again." For a few minutes, they play separately, and then they are back sharing their toys with each other. The columnist remarks to another mother, "How do children do that? How do they manage to be so angry with each other one minute and the best of friends the next?" And the mother answers, "It's easy. They choose happiness over righteousness."

We too have the power to choose happiness over righteousness. Righteousness means remembering every time someone hurt us or disappointed us and never letting them forget it. And not only that, giving them the right to remember every time we hurt them or let them down and constantly remind us of it. Happiness means giving people the right to be human—to be weak, selfish, and occasionally forgetful—and realizing that we have no alternative to living with imperfect people.

The quest for righteousness estranges people from each other; the quest for happiness enables them to get past their shortcomings and connect with each other. And strange as it may seem, happiness may be a more authentically religious value than righteousness.

During the course of the year, I see many people who come with diverse burdens—difficulties in managing their lives, in coping, in communicating. Sometimes I am a facilitator, sometimes a counselor; sometimes, all I can do is offer a sympathetic ear. But the most poignant and intractable problems are conflicts that arise in the relationship between people who should love each other and not hate each other.

I was discussing funeral services for a father who was survived by two sons. When I asked the son who was making the arrangements, "Where will the family sit shivah?" I was requested to make no public announcement, because the sons would not sit together in one house. The reason? Their wives stopped talking to each other years ago over some invitation which was not reciprocated. At least, that is what he thought it was. By now, he was not quite sure what had caused the split in the family. He could not remember precisely the source of the conflict, but whatever it was, neither brother could forget or forgive.

Extreme case, one says. Perhaps. But is there anyone who hasn't, in the course of the year, experienced anger and hurt elicited by those who are closest to him? The relationships of brothers and sisters, of friends and relatives, of business and professional associates—all of these, no matter how seemingly strong and enduring, are in reality fragile indeed. They can be disrupted or shattered by a thoughtless word, an unkind deed, a gesture or symbol that is perceived as a hostile act. When we become offended, we feel hurt, and we respond with anger and vindictiveness, even in our most cherished relationships.

What then is the power of forgiveness? Forgiveness is the courage to move on and not be caught in the bitterness of the past. Forgiveness is the courage to see the whole person rather than focus on the bad.

Forgiveness is about remembering the kindnesses that someone did for us during their lifetime, not the errors they made. Forgiveness is the ability to understand that people change and mature. Forgiveness is also about changing our own attitudes and thoughts about one another.

Forgiveness is not about turning the other cheek only to be slapped again. Forgiveness is about letting go of fear, of hurt, and of pain.

Forgiveness is about moving on with life. It teaches us that life is too short and too precious to live in the past and not enjoy today.

Forgiveness is about changing our attitude. A healthy personality finds the courage to move on and will not be caught in the bitterness of the past.

Several years ago, I offered my own version of a guaranteed weight loss program. Unlike other highly touted diet plans, mine did not require giving up any of the foods people love to eat. I simply suggested that if people were to lay aside a grudge or forgive someone, they would feel as though they were ten pounds lighter.

Sometime later, a congregant called and said, "My brother and I had an argument several months ago. I have been waiting for him to be the one who called to apologize. I wasn't going to make the first move. Then I remembered something you said, and I realized how foolish I was to let my pride prevent me from reaching out to him. Suddenly, it made sense to get rid of the animosity which was weighing me down."

A psychologist published a study about the dynamics of forgiveness. All the people whom he interviewed agreed on one point. When they forgave someone, when they let go of a grievance they had been carrying for some time, every single one of them experienced a physical sense of relief, a feeling of having put down a burden. They didn't realize they were carrying this load of bitterness until it was taken away from them.

Simon Weisenthal, the Nazi hunter, in the midst of his grim autobiography, tells one story in a lighter vein. There was a man living near him in one of the displaced persons camps after the war who borrowed ten dollars from him. He assured Weisenthal that he had a package coming from a relative any day and would possibly pay him back the next week. At week's end, he had an excuse for not paying, and the next week, he had an even better one. And so it went on for almost a year. Finally, one day the man came up to him with a ten dollar bill in his hand and said, "My visa has just come through. I'm leaving for Canada tomorrow. Here is the ten dollars I owe you." Weisenthal waved him away and said, "No, keep it. For ten dollars, it's not worth changing my opinion of you."

He was wrong, of course. It's a bargain to give away a grudge, a resentment for nothing. To get paid for getting rid of that burden is a double bargain.

It often seems that pride, which has the capacity to carry us to our greatest achievements, is the very same emotion that erects some of the most formidable barriers to forgiveness. Pride is the enemy of forgiveness. We all know someone who misses out on so much in life because of an unwillingness to be the first one to make a move.

Parents ask me, "Why should I be the one who takes the first step? Isn't it up to my child to say something first? Doesn't being a parent count for anything anymore?" My response: Love is too precious to be lost because of protocol. The tradition teaches that when people quarrel, the one who yields first is the greater of the two. When speaking with people who are facing the end of their life, rarely do I find them proud because they stubbornly stood on principle and refused to make a gesture which might have led to forgiveness. Far more common are the lamentations of those who understand at that time, better than ever before, that they sacrifice too much for the sake of their pride.

I plead for forgiveness even beyond this world—for death ends a life, but it does not end a relationship.

What remains can be either a blessing or a curse. While some are able to look back fondly on the life spent with a loved one, others carry the residue of pain left from years of suffering in a failed relationship. Long after the funeral, they continue to hear the echo of the words which wounded them. A lifetime of feelings lingers and refuses to disappear. I share with you this vignette, which makes this issue vivid and real.

Sarah, a mature woman, came to see me in an especially agitated state. Her fists clenched, her lips tight, Sarah was angry. She quickly came to the point. "Rabbi, my father died. I want to know what the Jewish law has to say. Do I have to recite the Kaddish?" At first I thought it was a gender question because in the Orthodox understanding of the Halakah, a woman does not recite the Kaddish and only male children observe the saying of the Kaddish. But I was wrong. The issue was not gender or Halakah. Sarah went on, "Do I really have to recite the Kaddish? I know the Kaddish is a prayer that honors the father. Well, I don't want to honor him because, Rabbi, he doesn't deserve it. And if I have to recite the Kaddish I will feel like a damned hypocrite."

She went on to pour out her heart about her father's coldness, callousness, and cruelty toward her and recounted episodes of his relentless carping criticism and abusiveness.

"Nothing about me was good; neither my appearance nor my dress nor my accomplishments. Every promise turned to ashes. I spent years in analysis to prop up my collapsing self-respect. If I now have to recite the Kaddish and sit shivah for him it would be a week of lies. Rabbi, what does the law say?"

There is a common notion that all the rabbi has to do to answer questions is to open up the Book of Codes to find the answer, "yes or no, permitted or forbidden." But Judaism is not a matter of the book and laws alone, Judaism also has to do with the heart and with relationships.

I looked at her. "Sarah, I feel your resentment. It is true that Kaddish is recited in honor of a parent. But for you, Sarah, the Kaddish you recite is not for the father you lost but for the father you never found. You recite Kaddish for the father who could have been and should have been but was not."

With that, Sarah's fists unclenched, tears welled up in her eyes, and her mood changed visibly. It changed from anger to sadness, from a desire to retaliate, to avenge her mistreatment, to something quieter, sadder, a recognition of an unhappy past. She brought up her jealousy of her elder brother, whom she perceived as being favored by her father. Sarah spoke freely now. All kinds of things spilled out.

At one point, I interrupted her and asked if she had known her father's father. She sat back and told me that her father's father was as mean and deprecating to his son as her father was to her. Then she smiled sadly. "I guess my father had my father for his father." She expressed a degree of sympathy for her father. Sarah left the study different from the daughter who came in. By the time we had ended, she had touched upon a full gamut of emotions: guilt, shame, jealousy, vindictiveness, love, and hope.

The emotional thread that binds so many of us together is the pain of living with a broken relationship and the never-dying hope that perhaps a new beginning is still possible. I quote from a letter submitted by a woman to Ann Landers. She wrote,

I have suddenly become aware that the years are flying by. Time somehow seems more precious. My parents suddenly seem old. My aunts and uncles are sick. I haven't seen some of my cousins for several years. Then, my thoughts turned to the dark side. I remember the feelings I have hurt and I recall my own hurt feelings—the misunderstandings and the unmended fences that separated us inside of barriers.

I think of my mother and her sister, who haven't spoken to each other in five years. As a result of their argument, my cousin and I haven't spoken either. What a waste of precious time. I am sure that there are millions of people in your audience who could tell similar stories.

Wouldn't it be terrific if a special day could be set aside to reach out and make amends? We would call it Reconciliation Day. Everyone would vow to write a letter or make a phone call and mend the strain that broke the relationship. It would also be the day on which we would all agree to accept the olive branch extended by a former friend. This day can be the starting point. We could go on from here to heal the wounds in our hearts and rejoice with a brand new beginning.

We have such a day. It is known as Yom Kippur.

Certainly it is hard to forgive past insults, hurts, cruelty. The story is told of two feuding congregants who had a long-standing hatred for each other over an ancient wrong. The rabbi, after great difficulty, finally succeeded in bringing them together for reconciliation. But the period of peace proved rather fragile. One man extended his hand and said to his opponent, "For the New Year, I wish you everything you wish for me." The second responded heatedly, "You see, Rabbi, he's starting up again."

Do we want this day to have a lasting impact on our lives? Then we must cultivate the gift of forgiveness.

I would like to see all Jews end Yom Kippur significantly lighter than they began it. Not because they will have gone a whole day without eating. That's a very temporary change. I'd like to see them lighter because they will have divested themselves of the burdens of bearing grudges, resentments, stale and outdated feuds based on misunderstandings that happened recently or years ago. And like everyone else who has given up a grudge, they'll be astonished by the sense that a burden has been lifted. They'll never know how weighted down they have been until they have released it.

Consider the story of Elizabeth Kenny, the Australian nurse who originated a method of treating polio. Once she was asked how she managed to stay so cheerful. "I suppose you were just born calm and smiling," said her friend. Sister Kenny laughed and said, "Oh, no, as a girl, I often lost my temper, but one day, when I became angry at a friend over a trivial matter, my mother said to me, 'Elizabeth, anyone

who angers you, conquers you.' And I have never forgotten her words."
What a brilliant insight. Sooner or later, our anger takes control of us;
our grudge becomes our obsession.

Anger is frustration turned inward. Anger, usually directed toward
others, harms only the one who is angry. It diminishes us, making us
appear petty, petulant. The Talmud teaches that one who is angry forgets his learning and makes a fool of himself. Let go of anger? It is easier said than done. Okay, don't let go of anger. Hold on to it. Nurture it.
Make it grow. Maintain that rage and fire in the belly against the ex-
spouse who just walked on you after all those years. And while you are
at it, make certain that the children learn to be angry as well. Teach
them to take on your rage and your indignation. Raise your children to
be cynical; tell them not to trust their better instincts. Empower them
to fight off anything that elicits love or commitment to another, because
that's what anger, well taught, most certainly does. Let go of the anger
because anger will never make a negative positive. The Midrash
teaches, "When a kettle boils, it spills hot water down its side." So, we
boil over with anger and we scald ourselves. Anger never makes things
better. We delude ourselves into thinking that with anger, we take control. In fact, because of anger, we lose all control. Anger does not free
us—it keeps us trapped in a cage of our own making. That is why Yom
Kippur is so important. It tells us in no uncertain terms, "Let it go. Let
go of anger at others and let go of the fire that rages within." As we ask
of God, "Selach Lanu," so too do we ask of ourselves that we may let go
of that which keeps us isolated from the best aspects of ourselves. May
we let go of the need to exact vengeance which can never be, so as to be
able to find a sense of peace and kindness, not only for others but for
the one who needs it most, ourselves.

Forgive others and rid yourself of the anger and hurt that seethe
within and embitter your life.

Forgive others by turning away from the anguish of the past and turn
instead to the work of fashioning a new and brighter future.

In this way, we shall be worthy of God's promise on this day of holiness: "Salachti Kidvorecha"—"I have forgiven, as you have asked."

FUTURE

The past is for wisdom, the present for action, but for joy, the future.

—RABBI ALORY DISRAELI, 1833

There is hope for your future.

—JEREMIAH 31.17

Is the Best Yet to Be?

For centuries, the liturgy of Rosh Hashanah and Yom Kippur has been replete with prayers for life. Untold generations, including our own, have repeated time and time again, "Zochraynu l'chayim melech chafetz bachayim"—"Remember us unto life, oh King who desires life." What greater fulfillment of this prayer than the benediction of long life—the supreme blessing of God? The Book of Proverbs states, "The aged head is a crown of glory." The older a person gets, in the traditional view, the more understanding and wisdom he acquires, and the more honor and veneration are due him. Old age is a reward. It is a privilege. It is the best part of life. Thus did Robert Browning, in his celebrated poem "Rabbi Ben Ezra," declare, "Come grow old along with me / the best is yet to be."

Our prayers have remained virtually unchanged, but a revolution has taken place in the world with regard to aging. For the greater part of recorded history, the aged possessed all authority and were accorded the greatest honor. The rabbis explain that the Hebrew word for old, "zaken," means "Zeh shekanah hokmah"—"He who has acquired wisdom." The position of the aged in the ancient world is summarized by a verse in Job: "With the aged is wisdom, and with length of days, understanding."

But the authority of the aged, like so many other traditional values, has been overthrown in our time. The aged have been toppled from the throne. Youth and youthfulness are considered the highest forms of being. To be old is to suffer from a disease for which there is no cure, to have a punishment for which there is no reprieve, to be an alien for whom there will be no welcome. As Dr. Abraham Joshua Heschel once said, "Old age is something we are all anxious to attain. However, once attained, we consider it a defeat, a form of capital punishment. In enabling us to reach old age, medical science may think that it gave us a blessing; however, we continue to act as if it were a disease."

Now this phenomenon is one that ought to engage our attention, for we face a paradoxical problem. The advance of medical science has increased our life expectancy. At the same time, the likelihood is increased that we will undergo impairment, rejection, and unhappiness as we enter the years of advanced age. The increased longevity of men and women is far from being the unqualified blessing for which the generations have prayed. It has turned out to be, with bitter irony, an embarrassment, a problem, sometimes a curse. Some statistics may be instructive at this point. Nearly thirty-three million Americans are at least sixty years old, and their number is growing by five hundred thousand a year, at twice the rate of our total population. They constitute the single largest minority in the nation—more belong to the category of "aged" than to any nonwhite racial group in the United States.

As recently as 1900, the life expectancy in the United States was less than fifty. Today it has risen to almost seventy. Reflection of this trend is found in the emergence of a new science called geriatrics, which is concerned exclusively with the aging process and its attendant problems. Geriatrics is the answer of science to mankind's perennial prayer. We all want to live long, but none of us want to be "old." Geriatrics tries to satisfy both contradictory desires simultaneously.

When does old age begin? Leo Rosten said it's when all the policemen look young, when the steps get steeper and the print gets smaller. We tend to define old age differently, depending on whose age we're talking about, our own or our neighbor's. Most of us seem to grow old about fifteen years later than the people we know. Moreover, we do not grow old uniformly. Different parts of the body do not age at the same pace. A physician may discover that a sixty-year-old man has a fifty-year-old kidney, a forty-year-old heart, and a seventy-year-old liver, while he may be trying to live a thirty-year-old life. Perhaps the best definition of old age is the one that Walter Reuther was fond of quoting. He said, "It's when you're too old to work and too young to die."

The greatest and most universal fear in our society is the fear of getting old. It is the pervasive American obsession. As the years advance, we tend to make little jokes about birthdays, and we begin to understand why Jack Benny remained a perpetual thirty-nine. This morbid fear of aging has given birth to a new vocabulary of euphemism. At a time when four-letter words, formerly considered taboo, are now uttered without reticence, not only in private conversation but in almost all social settings, I find it curious and remarkable that a certain word is still suppressed. The word is *old*. We do not speak of old age. We talk of "golden years." If the phrase weren't so sad, it would be ludicrous. We do not organize old age groups. We create "golden age clubs." We now recognize a class of Americans that we call "senior citizens." Does that make the rest of us "junior citizens"? The subject of old age is not addressed directly in American life.

But the problems of aging will not go away—because they are real—and history provides no guide. If the past offers any insight at all into this matter, it is this. In the best of premodern societies, old age was not separated from the rest of the life span. A generation or two ago, grandparents lived with their families as honored members of the household. They were able to exert beneficent influence upon the lives not only of their own children but also of their grandchildren, serving as a symbol of the continuity of time and tradition.

Some of us have been profoundly influenced by having known our grandparents in the constancy of a family unit. This experience in our times grows increasingly uncommon. There are homes for the aged, hotels for senior citizens, retirement villages for the elderly. All these meet that need which arises out of the conditions we associate with age. The aged do not fit into the lifestyle of the contemporary family, and they know it. Thus do we find a remarkable paradox. We pray for long life, and if our prayers are answered, we are miserable.

How do we escape from this impasse? We fight against old age; we pretend it does not exist. We conceal our age; we hide our years; we choose the youthful style in apparel, in fashion, in the aspects of popular culture. On the dance floor, we vie with the youngsters doing the most violent of dances, which leave us limp and exhausted. I'm not criticizing these tactics as wrong. They are praiseworthy when they are in proportion.

Medical authorities have pointed out that the efforts of people in middle years and beyond to remain young have a beneficial effect upon their physical health and reduce the incidence of certain conditions and diseases of old age. There is no reason why we should surrender to age without a struggle. Fighting against illness and declining powers, holding fast to our interest and joy in life—these are worthy of great praise. Enjoyment of life is perhaps the greatest mitzvah because in cherishing life, we are expressing gratitude to God, the Giver of life.

But sooner or later we will be forced to admit that we are not as young as we used to be. And we don't want to hear this because we are afraid—afraid of the physical and psychological effects that age will have upon us; afraid of the inevitable loss of status that will accompany our retirement; afraid of our loss of independence; afraid of being left alone, rejected, and abandoned.

As a response to that fear, one finds that anger and resentment toward the old are on the rise. It is as though the aged are an alien race to which the rest of us will never belong.

A new term has been coined: *ageism*, contempt for and discrimination against the aged. This bigotry is rapidly becoming as serious a problem as racism, but with this curious difference. It is very unlikely that we shall ever become black, but we may all grow old. We may become the victims of the very forces of discrimination and exclusion that we aid and abet.

The Jewish tradition is clear, unequivocal, and insistent on our responsibility for the aged. Created in the image of God, the aged deserve not only love and compassion but also reverence. The biblical pronouncement to "honor the face of the aged" does not have an asterisk with the designation "only if he has financial resources, or children that are able and willing to pay the expense, or if he still has mental faculties or a pleasant disposition." The Bible says, "Honor the face of the aged." The elderly person's accumulation of years is the only qualification he needs to merit this honor.

Older Americans are not a homogeneous group. They come in all shapes and sizes, with all kinds of needs and capabilities. The only common denominator is that virtually all of them are in one way or another disadvantaged. There are the physically disadvantaged—the millions who are feeble and ill with not enough money for adequate housing, medical care, food, clothing, transportation.

There's another category—millions of older Americans who are psychically disadvantaged. They are healthy and reasonably well off but have been segregated from the rest of society by the accident of calendar age. They are eager, competent, and willing to serve; they seek to exercise their abilities and talents, but they are denied such opportunities.

The author James Michener put this issue into clear focus when he wrote, "The problem of caring for the aged looms as the principal social problem of the balance of the century, greater than ecological asphyxiation, greater than over-population, greater than the energy crisis."

What is the situation with regard to the Jewish aged in our own community? The Jewish aged in Detroit number nine thousand. However, this number will not remain constant but will rise, by the 1990s, to thirteen thousand. At the present time, the aged constitute 12 percent of our population. In ten years, they will be 15 percent. These figures do not take into account those already in institutions. Compare this to 1900, when the elderly represented 3 percent of the population. At present, those over fifty comprise 43 percent of the entire Jewish population, as compared to 30 percent of other Americans. As a community, our birthrate is lower than that of other Americans, which will push the percentage of elderly to ever higher levels.

Another important statistic must be considered. Seventy-two per-cent of the Jewish poor—those who earn less than four thousand dol-lars a year—are in the over-sixty-five age category. A high correlation exists between being old and being poor.

As a community, we have a responsibility to provide care and service for our aged and to plan for increased budgets. Certain fundamental needs must be met—adequate food, better housing, and health care. Very often older people require services that can enable them to be integrated into their community without institutional care. However the institutional facilities and the range of services presently provided for the Jewish aged in our community are not adequate to meet the need. Adequate resources have not been allocated; the processes of planning and funding have not kept pace with the demand. Plans are presently being formulated for expanding the institutional capacity of the home for the aged, for building new facilities, and for providing additional services to the aged in our Jewish community. I urge that this effort be deemed of the highest priority for our Jewish community. We must concentrate our energies and mobilize our resources for this sacred and urgent task.

On the personal level, we should foster programs of education in which all of us become more aware about, more sensitive to, the physi-cal and psychological aspects of aging. I was told about a course taught at the University of Michigan's Institute of Gerontology designed to show people who work with the elderly how to change their environ-ment to make it safe and more pleasant. Each of the students was given a pair of eyeglasses that had been treated with an opaque coating to simulate the normal changes that occur in the human eye as it ages. For two hours these students saw Ann Arbor through the eyes of a seventy-five-year-old person. They experienced that which they had not yet grasped. They understood why old people seem confused and nervous when they cross the street or walk down a sidewalk. They felt the frus-trations of older people who have difficulties in depth or color percep-tion or in recognizing faces.

We need to rethink our national priorities. America provides relatively little funding for research in aging. The amount invested in such research equals 1/25 the cost of a fighter-bomber, or about eight cents per person per year.

But what about us? What is our responsibility to ourselves? I think our situation is expressed by an elderly Jewish gentleman who went to his doctor. He complained of a variety of aches and pains and described them in great detail. His doctor examined him, and then he resolved to confront his patient with the facts of life. He said, "Look, Zadeh, you're almost ninety. What do you expect? I can't make you any younger." "Nu, I don't want you should make me younger—make me older."

We have no acceptable alternative to aging. We are resigned to undergo the process that aging will bring, but we need to think and plan about the kind of life we want for ourselves if we are to discover that "the best is yet to be." Without the purposefulness that comes from self-knowledge and self-awareness, we are likely to experience the decline of our powers with the passage of the years, rather than a "crown of glory."

I offer the following suggestions.

1. Though we may now be under thirty, it is not too soon to begin thinking about and preparing for the years following retirement. Retirement often seems to mean the end of a man's productive life, much as the marriage of a woman's youngest child may convey to her a feeling that her usefulness is ended. In general, retirement should be treated with great caution. Four out of ten men, in a recent survey, indicated they were involuntarily retired. I know many people who have worked all their lives without any thought of someday retiring. And now they have leisure time and are unprepared for it, so instead of enjoying their leisure years, they curse their emptiness, nurse their various and diverse ailments, and live in the past. Individuals who make the most successful adjustment to retirement and the inevitable changes brought on by aging are those who have vital interests, who are open to new ideas, new horizons, new experiences.

2. It is never too late to begin. Contrary to popular opinion, age has little to do with ability to learn new things or to adjust to new situations. A neurologist once wrote, "At sixty the body has certainly passed beyond its greatest strength, and physical demands should be lessened and changed. But the brain quite often is ready for its best performance in certain fields."

A recent analysis of the achievements of four hundred famous people revealed that more than one-third achieved their greatest accomplishments after the age of sixty. Twenty-three percent scored their greatest success in life after the age of seventy. Examples? George Bernard Shaw was still writing in his nineties, while Verdi created his Othello and Falstaff at the ages of seventy-four and eighty. Toscanini was conducting in his eighties. Grandma Moses became a painter when most artists would retire. Pope John XXIII ascended the throne of the Vatican in his seventy-eighth year and transformed the Catholic Church.

We Jews can look with pride at some amazing achievements of older people. Ben-Gurion in his eighties was still dynamic and inspiring. Golda Meir continues to exercise her influence in Israel and elsewhere. Professor Mordecai Kaplan is in his nineties and still continues to write and lecture as he presents his challenging ideas.

Justice Oliver Wendell Holmes once put it, "To be seventy years young is sometimes more cheerful and hopeful than to be forty years old." You may argue that these examples are of the famous, the distinguished, and the brilliant. The *New York Times* recently featured a survey of continuing education which summarized in a number of articles the experiences of older students who have entered the world of the university. There was an article by Harry Gersch, who described his year after having entered Harvard as a freshman at the age of sixty-three—a year of challenge, of occasional frustration, but of intellectual stimulation and achievement.

As long as we keep our minds open and alert, as long as we are willing to try a new skill, entertain a new thought, surrender an old prejudice—so long do we remain vital people.

A minister, on meeting a little boy, asked, "Who made you?" "Well, to tell you the truth," the little boy replied, "I ain't done yet." There are

mountaintops to reach. There are dreams to fulfill and visions to realize. I have seen older people who welcome new challenges and who set
new goals. They summon the motivation and the strength not to complete the work, which is impossible, but never to desist from it.

3. We should return to the sources of our faith—faith in God, faith
in the world, faith in life, faith in ourselves. The best way to overcome
our fear of growing old is to renew our faith in our Creator and in the
wisdom of His plan for life. Consider what it would mean if it were true
that youth is the happiest time of life. If that were so, then nothing
would be sadder to look at than a young person of twenty-five, for here
we would see someone who had reached the very peak of existence and
now could only expect decay, decline, and descent into the valley. I cannot think of any opinion that is a greater insult to the human personality and to the human spirit.

If we are to face the advancing years with serenity and hope, we
ought to realize that God has arranged human life on an ascending
scale. Every age has its unique satisfactions and joys, just as every hour
in the day has its own charm and loveliness. Being a father, I know, is
wonderful. My older friends tell me that being a grandfather is too. And
I suspect that being a great-grandfather may be even more exciting. We
ought to cultivate, now, faith in God and trust in the reasonableness of
His work, the faith that will enable us to find wisdom and courage for
all the years that lie ahead.

None of us is so young that he can postpone the preparation for the
years of harvest. And none is so old that he cannot capture their joy. If
we learn how to grow in knowledge, if we affirm our capacity for life, if
we renew our faith, we shall attain wisdom greater than learning, contentment richer than wealth. We have been offered an invitation which
Robert Browning placed in the mouth of Rabbi Ben Ezra, an invitation
not without risk of pain or sorrow but which bears, nevertheless, a glorious celebration of all human existence: "Come, grow old along with
me / the best is yet to be / the last of life, for which the first was made."

The Challenge of Freedom

I heard a story of a Russian commandant who comes to America to visit a factory. He takes a tour and looks into the product, the height of American ingenuity. Suddenly, he hears a whistle, and the workers start to leave. The Russian gets upset. "Hurry, stop them. They're escaping." The factory owner answers, "Don't worry, it's only the lunch whistle. They'll be back." An hour later, the whistle sounds again, and the workers all return. The Russian is amazed. The factory owner turns to the Russian. "So what about our product?" "Never mind the product. I'll take one of those whistles."

The "shofar" is like that factory whistle. When it blows, Jews return to their tradition.

In the Book of Life, may we be remembered and inscribed before Thee. We, and all thy people, the House of Israel—for life and for peace.

The recurring theme of these Holidays is a plea for life, a hope for inscription in the Book of Life.

Is it logical to pray for something that will someday be denied us? Since each of us owes life one death, there will come the time, inevitably, when our prayers will be rejected, our hopes denied.

Is it not possible that what is reflected in these prayers for life is not so much a hope for another volume of life as a desire to strengthen our will to live? Perhaps these prayers express not so much our fear of death as our fear that our will to live may falter, our fear that we may lose our enthusiasm for living.

The dictionary provides several definitions of life. "Life is the quality which distinguishes a vital and functioning being from a dead one." That is glorious, but it's not a lot of help. There is another one. It says, "the period of usefulness of something." I thought, If usefulness is the determinant of our being alive or dead, then there are an awful lot of dead people running around the place. The one I especially cherish is the third definition: "To pass through or spend the duration." Most of us are really passing through and spending the duration. Yet most of us are, in the real sense of the word, alive and living fully.

I am reminded of a verse read at the last Sabbath of the year.

"Behold, I set before you this day, life and good, death and evil; you shall choose life." Note well how the Torah puts it. The choice of life is not natural and automatic. Man must be commanded to choose it.

How do we choose life? It is by living to the fullest of our capacities.

Here is a true story of a business leader who chose life for thousands of his employees. His name is Aaron Feurestein, and he is president of the family company, Malden Mills, that manufactures a popular fabric, Polartec. He is an observant Jew whose conduct is shaped by the values of the Jewish tradition. In December, an uncontrollable fire at the mill burned most of his company and put three thousand out of work when Americans were spending freely at the Christmas season. Seventy years old at the time, Aaron Feuerstein rushed to the inferno and announced he would not take the insurance money and retire, thereby leaving his workers to fend for themselves. Following the Talmudic aphorism "Where there are no men, be a man," he declared he would rebuild and, in the meantime, would pay every worker and continue to provide their health insurance.

When a reporter asked why he did not just take his money and walk away from the shell of the mill and do the easy thing, Feurestein replied, "Because it wouldn't be right." Feuerstein went home to observe the Sabbath, declaring that the same God who inhabits his home presides over his business and informs all that he does. The mill was in Lawrence, Massachusetts. The mayor; the governor; two senators; and finally, the president of the United States were awed by his attitude and commitment. The mill workers, impressed by the relationship between his actions and his religion, blessed him as an angel. Here was a man who chose life for himself and for a whole community.

So, the Jewish tradition tells us to say "yes" to life. "Yes" to wonder, to joy, even to pain. Instead of hopeless, try "possible," try "hopeful," try "I will."

The great scholar Raba declared that when scholars would say farewell, they used these words: "May He who gives life to the living give you a long, good, and happy life."

We speak of God in our prayers as giving life to the dead. What is the meaning of the phrase that God gives life not to the dead but to the living? The intriguing idea is that it is possible to be alive and yet not live. God can perform the miracle of bringing the living back to life. A professor at Columbia University, Nicholas Murray Butler, once said that he knew a man for whose tombstone he would like to propose the following inscription: "John Smith—Died at the age of 30—Buried at the age of 70."

Does God give life to the living? Doctors are beginning to discover that hope and faith have a positive effect on disease. Some of the most telling work has been done in Israel by two outstanding research scientists. They studied ten thousand men with the risk factors for angina pectoris—abnormal heart rhythms and high anxiety levels. The researchers used psychological tests and questionnaires to find out what other factors determined which men would actually develop the chest pains. The most consistent predictor of chest pains turned out to be a "no" answer to the question, "Does your wife show you her love?" Insurance companies have found that if a wife kisses her husband goodbye in the morning, he has fewer auto accidents and lives five years longer.

There is yet another way to choose life. To be inscribed in the Book of Life is a prayer not only for ourselves but for the entire Household of

Israel. We are commanded to choose life for the Jewish people because we have had substantial achievement that bears witness to our will to live. This year, when we sound the shofar at the end of Yom Kippur, we shall usher in the fiftieth year since Israel's independence, Israel's jubilee year, an appropriate occasion to remind ourselves of what Israel has meant to and done for the Jewish people. For two thousand years, our people were the most persecuted and despised on the face of the globe. We suffered indignity, ghettos, pogroms, inquisitions, the Holocaust. And now, in this generation, we have seen Jewish history turned upside down because there is a State of Israel for the first time in two thousand years. Despite ongoing anti-Semitism and despite the still very real threats to Israel's survival, we as a people are prouder and stronger and more secure than any other people on the face of the globe. Whether you are Kurdish or Russian or Ethiopian, or whatever—you're safest and luckiest if you are also Jewish.

For two thousand years, Jews were hunted. Jews had to hide for their lives. Today, not only do Jews have a safe haven, but they have the power to rescue others. For centuries, Jews were at the mercy of others. Today, Jews are the secure ones and have the ability to come out of the sky and save others. For the first time in two thousand years, Jews are the rescuers, not the rescued. And all because there is a State of Israel. Let us rejoice in the miracle.

And yet, we Jews in America are deeply anxious about our future. Will we endure; will we continue? A keen observer of the American Jewish scene begins his lecture by telling his audience the definition of a Jewish telegram. It reads, "Start worrying. Letter follows immediately." We worry about our survival and anti-Semitism and Israel and assimilation and continuity. We have worried for so long that we now suffer from a collective sense of Jewish failure and foreboding. Something deep inside of us wants us to believe that our great days are behind us, that we may be coming to the end of the Jewish people. And we have reason for this fear. Because we count too few who care, because we are not pleased with the quality of Jewish life, because we are worried about our youth, because we find nothing but assimilation.

I was recently asked to write an article for a Jewish journal on the subject "What will the Jewish community look like twenty-five years from now?" I responded by explaining that it would indeed be foolish to try to predict the future, for it will be forged out of circumstances and realities that we cannot possibly anticipate today.

But there is one thing about the Jewish future of which I have no doubt. There will be one. And twenty-five years from now, the Jewish community may be more vital than it is today. How can I be so sure? Haven't I read the studies and statistics on assimilation and alienation? How could I ignore the very real threats to peace in the Middle East and the challenges to Jewish education and Jewish literacy here in America?

I believe that we can identify our problem and find solutions that will transform the character of American Jewry.

Having read all the reports and studies that anticipate our demise, I still hope for a brighter future for our people. The problem with the doomsayers is that they are too focused on the future. My optimism comes from the wisdom of the past.

I have learned from the long and arduous history of our people that our very existence is most improbable—that by all the laws of history, we should have disappeared a millennium ago. We have made it to the present because we have refused to be defeated by cynicism and discouragement.

Many observers reject my optimistic views. I once told my wife, Leypsa, that I am an incurable optimist. Her response: "By now, you should be cured."

What is our fear? The pessimists say that Jews are discarding their heritage and opting out in record numbers. The American Jewish community—the most vibrant, diverse, productive, creative, and powerful Diaspora Jewish community in history—believes it is under siege. My text is not the Bible or the Talmud. It is rather a thirty-page essay in *New York Magazine* on July 14, entitled "Are American Jews Disappearing—Are American Jews Assimilating Themselves out of Existence?" A group of Jewish leaders and academicians of diverse backgrounds are quoted and discussed. Consider this representative voice: "Our grandparents prayed for a melting pot, but what we have now is a melt down." He goes on to say, "There are no barking dogs and no Zykon-B gas, but make no mistake: this is a spiritual Holocaust."

A word of history. For most of this century, American Jews have been obsessed with becoming good citizens, with blending in and succeeding in a competitive American society, and, for many, their rise to success was phenomenal. Jews hold two seats on the Supreme Court, 10 percent of the Senate, five of eight Ivy League presidencies. The following story provides an interesting perspective on success.

Three men were arguing about the meaning of success in life. The first man said, "I know what success is. It is when the president of the United States invites you to lunch in the White House."

The second replied, "That is nothing. Success is when you are having lunch with the president of the United States, the hot line from Russia rings, and the president says to the Russian premier, 'I can't talk to you right now. I have someone here for lunch.'"

The third replied, "That is nothing. Success is when you are having lunch with the president of the United States, the hot line from Russia rings, and the president answers the phone, turns to you, and says, 'It's for you.'"

Some of us have almost achieved that level of success. But now the question is, Can we embrace modernity in an open society and live fully engaged Jewish lives?

Dr. Egon Mayer, a noted social scientist, says nothing could be more disastrous to the future of Jewry than self-fulfilling despair. Nor is any attitude less warranted.

I quote: "I call this fear that Jews are disappearing the Houdini Syndrome. It crops up periodically. But it hasn't happened in three thousand years, so it is difficult to take seriously. In 1964, *Look* magazine ran a cover story called 'The Vanishing American Jew.' It was prophetic. What happened was that *Look* magazine vanished.

"The ultimate question is can you have a Jewish community if it doesn't have some elements of a distinctive culture? And can you have the elements of a distinctive culture given the immense power of popular culture and the weakness of Jewish life?" Is there any basis for hope?"

A few years back, Montana State had a bad football season. But Coach Jenkins faced the New Year optimistically. "We are sure to improve," he said. "We lost all ten games last season. This year we have only nine games scheduled." My hope is based on different circumstances.

I believe that there is nothing inevitable about the crisis of Jewish identity in the Diaspora. It is the result of a century of bad, if understandable, decisions. One above all—we neglected Jewish education. The result is that so many of us know little about Judaism and their children know less.

They know about the Holocaust—about how Jews died, not how they lived. They know about Israel, but that is somewhere else, not here. They know about anti-Semitism, but that is no reason to want their children to be exposed to it. They know about Jewish humor and food. By now, so do non-Jews.

Collectively, we made the mistake our whole history should have warned us against. From earliest times, Jews predicated their survival on education. Moses commanded us to teach our children diligently. Throughout the Middle Ages, education was the first priority in every Jewish community's budget.

There is no other way. The survival of a minority is a matter of nurture, not nature. It is sustained through education. So long as Jews learned, they lived.

We know what works best outside the classrooms—Israel experiences, outreach programs, family education, camping. We need to frame a network of positive Jewish experiences aimed at parents no less than at children.

Without education, we relied on nostalgia. A sense of Jewishness survives for three generations on memories alone. So long as Jews could remember *Bubbe* and *Zeida* with their Yiddish and Yiddishkeit, they stayed Jews. But our children belong to the fourth generation. For them, Jewishness cannot be remembered; it must be created.

We are given the responsibility of engaging the mind and touching the heart of the Jewish child. Let there be no misunderstanding of the condition of Jews in a free society. We are free to choose, and especially our children and grandchildren are free to choose, as our ancestors did in days of yore, whether to accept or not accept the Torah. Sometimes they choose to turn away from their heritage.

In an old Zen parable, a man goes searching for a lost object. He is crawling on his hands and knees when a friend approaches him. "What are you doing?" the friend asks. "I am looking for something that I lost," he replied. "Where did you lose it?" the friend asked. "Over there," said the man, pointing to a place far from where they were. "Then why are you looking for it over here?" "Because the light is better here," the man replied.

In the search for the holy and the ultimate, many American Jews are looking in different and disparate places. They are looking in places where they have heard that the light is better: the New Age religion, diverse cults, messianic movements, Buddhism, Christianity. We need to return to our roots to become again *Beyt Yaakov,* the House of Jacob, a people that is rooted to history, memory, knowledge, and texts.

The story is told of the little girl who announced to her mother, "You know that beautiful vase on the parlor table, which you said has been handed down from generation to generation?"

"Yes," replied the mother, "what about it?" "Well," answered the little girl, "this generation just dropped it."

It is our responsibility to ensure for this generation and generations to come that we shall not drop the priceless heritage which our ancestors transmitted to us, their descendants.

Every year, I ask the confirmation class to set forth their beliefs about Judaism and the Jewish way of life. And one statement said so much in a very few words.

The student wrote, "The purpose of my Jewish education is to know who I am and for what I stand." That sixteen-year-old student shared with us a great insight. We want our children to know who they are, to identify with the glorious past of the Jewish people, to feel a common bond with Jews all over the world, to carry the name "Jew" with the full recognition that it represents a high privilege, as well as a great responsibility.

And we want them to know what they stand for. They stand for the highest moral values the world has ever grasped. They stand for the ideals of the Torah. And our young need to know that what they stand for is so important that God Himself has made them the guardians of the Torah.

The problem is not finding the way but creating the will. The critical change took place when Jews stopped thinking of themselves as the people loved by God and started seeing themselves as the people hated by Gentiles. One can want to hand the first on to one's children but not the second.

The issue is loyalty, but it's deeper than loyalty. A leading scholar declared, "You can't have people loyal to something they know nothing about." Jewish pride must be more than crowing over how many Nobel Prize winners we have. That kind of pride is rather empty. There has to be pride in tradition, history, destiny, language, and a way of living. That requires a real Jewish education. Jewish continuity will be achieved once education and outreach become our top priorities, receiving the best of our leadership and funding. And that will happen when, putting the ghosts of the past behind us, we relearn what our ancestors always knew: that being a Jew is not a fate but a privilege.

Undoubtedly, the rate of assimilation in America engenders pessimism with regard to our future.

But I remember the insight of a great rabbi of this century who said, "The righteous don't complain about evil, but add righteousness. They don't complain about heresy, but add faith. They don't complain about ignorance, but add wisdom." My response is, This is our task—to move beyond the complaint, to see beyond the forces of assimilation, and to discover the ways in which we can work for the renewal of Jewish life.

Moreover, I find a genuine hunger for Jewish values, tradition, and learning. And many of the most hungry are often the children of totally assimilated parents. Wherever someone has something genuine to say, young Jews are listening.

I believe that those who choose to remain Jewish or to become Jews are all the more committed. And this group of serious Jews is what Judaism has always been about.

There are many hopeful developments that we could identify which buttress our faith in the future of American Judaism. But I am afraid I might draw too optimistic a picture and be among those whom Jeremiah castigated "for healing the breach of my people lightly." The rabbi should be the last to proclaim all is well when, in fact, so much remains to be done. But these examples and more that could be cited are signs of what we might become, of the great spiritual potential which is ours.

There are great possibilities that lie before us.

We could make Jewish education for our youth accessible and universal.

We could develop models of learning and living for the Jewish home and family, as well as the classroom. Federations and synagogues need to join hands in addressing the urgent needs of Jewish life. Yes, we who believe in the eternity of the Jewish people can renew its life in this land of freedom.

When the Torah reader calls the first Aliyah, we all respond, "And you who cleave unto the Lord, your God, you are alive, every one of you on this day." Will American Jews disappear, or will they give birth to new life? Such a question was once confronted by a profound sage.

There was a traveling rabbi who had the ability to answer every question. Never once was he wrong. Then, one day, he came to a town where thousands came to hear him. One little girl raised her hand. "I have the question you can't answer," she said. "I have in my hand a bird. Tell me. Is this bird alive or dead?" She thought, If he says it's alive, I'll close my hand and kill the bird. If he says it's dead, I'll open my hand and let the bird live.

The rabbi, aware of the trick behind this question, was perplexed.

Here was the question he couldn't answer. But then, all at once, the answer hit him. Here, he knew, was the secret of Jewish destiny. Looking at the girl in the midst of the huge crowd, he said, "My precious, precious child, you hold in your hand a bird. You ask if it's alive or dead. I can only tell you one thing. The question of life and death lies in your hands."

We have choices. We can select faith over despair. We can choose life.

We seek zest for living. Who is the real atheist? The one who says there is no God? What does it matter what a person says with his lips? The real atheist is he who seeks no joy, no meaning, no challenge in life. We seek not to add years to our life but to add life to our years. Choose life!

The answer lies in our hands . . .

Remembering the Future

I call to mind a verse that is attributed to Moses, the leader of the Jewish people, who struggled to fulfill a mission for which he had not quite enough time. It was his task to liberate a people, to bring them across the wilderness, to represent to them the Torah, and to transform them into a holy nation. There was an incident recorded in the Book of Deuteronomy, an incident uniquely characteristic of the biblical tradition and the Jewish practice of engaging in debate with God. We talk to Him. We disagree with Him. We demand justice when we think we have been unjustly treated. This habit of ours of having arguments with God began with Abraham, our father. He questioned God's justice about destroying the cities of Sodom and Gomorrah. The biblical Book of Job is one powerful argument with God, and even in modern times, particularly among the great figures of the Hasidic movement, there are legends and stories that portray the Jewish claims against God.

This Torah portion to which I make reference is in the tradition of a classical lawsuit with God. Moses is pleading his case. He makes a particular demand on the basis of justice, and he says, talking to his people, "I made a plea with God in those days, and I said, 'Oh Lord, let me cross the Jordan. Let me enter the promised land.'"

Now that seems to be a just plea. It should surely have been granted.

Moses had started the whole process of deliverance, which began when he stood bravely before Pharaoh forty years earlier. He led that difficult and troublesome people for forty years in the wilderness. They frequently rebelled. They constantly grumbled. They even reverted to idolatry. He lived through it all and led them nearer to the promised land. Now, finally, at the very edge of the Jordan, when he wanted to complete his historic task, he is forbidden to do so. He wants to know: "What is the justice in having me die before I finish the one challenging enterprise to which I have dedicated my entire life?"

God responds like a stern, harsh judge and says in words that I do not recall occurring anywhere else in the Scriptures, a phrase never found in any other dialogue of man and God recorded in the Bible. God says to him, "Rav lacho"—"That is enough now. Stop." "Al tosef"—"Do not proceed further in this matter. Do not say anything more on this subject." God says, "I do not want to hear from you again about this at all." God silences him brusquely.

Why? Was Moses' plea so unjust? I have thought about that passage, and I believe that what seems to be unjust and unkind was not a cruel verdict but a powerful lesson. God wanted to indicate that this plea of Moses to finish the work that he had begun over forty years ago was not just. It seems just, but it isn't just. Because little tasks can be begun, continued, and finished. But the great tasks, the world tasks, are never completed. God's message was this: "You think your work will be completed if I allow you to go and cross the Jordan into the promised land? On Mount Sinai I gave you Ten Commandments to give to your people and to the world: Thou shalt not steal; thou shalt not kill. Have robbery and murder ceased in the world? Is the task of establishing law and order completed anywhere in the world? Such tasks are not easily finished. So don't talk to me about finishing your work. You are the first of the prophets. I have prepared successors. You will have a successor prophet named Isaiah, and Isaiah will say, 'The lion will lie down peaceable with the lamb' and 'They will turn their swords into plowshares.' Has that work been finished? When will the world be in perfect peace? So 'rav lacho,' stop. You are working on too great a cause for you to demand to see it completed in your day. It is not small enough, limited enough, precise enough to be finished in one lifetime."

Moses agreed. He accepted this decision against him, because we do not find him arguing beyond this point. But he felt that he ought to have some sort of consolation. And in the next verse, God gives it to him. He says, "Go up to the summit of Mount Pisgah and look westward. See the Sharon Valley. See the Great Sea beyond. See it with your own eyes."

What kind of consolation is that? Actually, it's one of the basic consolations in life.

If you can stand on a higher level and continue to see the promised land in spite of the day-to-day heartbreak, the day-to-day frustrations, the day-to-day disappointments, that is one of the grandest spiritual achievements a person can attain. In spite of all the crime and the corruption and the violence, domestic and international, and the threat of violence, we believe, because of Moses, and because of Isaiah, and because of all the teachers of Judaism, that there is a promised land. And we have mountaintops from which we can look out and acquire this vision. That's the Jewish will to believe, because if the heart continues to have faith, the soul will continue to strive for goodness.

The Talmud declares that when a man stands before the final judgment, he is going to be asked certain questions. First: Have you conducted your business affairs honestly? Honesty, integrity—that's the first, the fundamental, question. Second: Have you fixed regular hours for study? This question is asked by a religion that considers the development of the mind as a tribute to God who gave us intelligence. Third: Have you maintained your faith in the salvation of mankind, in redemption? You have to struggle; you have to persevere to believe that beyond the Jordan there is still the promised land. Such faith has to be fought for. It's not easy in the face of bitter reality to hold on to such a resplendent vision of the future. But God aids man to maintain that faith.

And finally, in the same passage, God says to Moses, "Now there's Joshua, your disciple. Speak to him; give him courage. He will not finish either—no one will finish the great career of this eternal people—but he will carry it further. He will bring them across the Jordan."

This is the other great consolation in life. To know that there is another generation that will continue your work. There will be another generation to cherish our dreams and to realize our aspirations.

As we begin marking this 120th year, I have thought about seventeen Jews who organized Shaarey Zedek Society in 1861. The story of Moses and his quest resonates with their act of faith. They could not have foreseen that the small, struggling congregation that they established would one day comprise a membership of eighteen hundred and achieve prominence not only in this city and state but throughout the nation. A hundred and twenty years ago there were less than fifty thousand Jews all over the United States, which represented fewer than two-tenths of 1 percent of the total population.

That small group of founders and the several generations that immediately followed could not have foreseen the transforming changes in the history of American Jewry: the mass migration of Jews from eastern Europe to the New World, the growth and development of the American Jewish community, the Holocaust and the destruction of European Jewry, the creation of the State of Israel, the tenacity of Soviet-Jewish identity, the resurgence of Jewish ethnicity in America.

But they did know that their synagogue, which met in those days in a rented hall on the second floor above a drugstore on what is now Cadillac Square, did not begin in Detroit but had its origins twenty-five hundred years earlier when a group of Jewish exiles in Babylonia established a synagogue as a permanent part of Jewish life. And they also knew their congregation was a witness to their generation, their community, their determination to live as Jews. It was a declaration of faith in the heritage of their fathers and also, no less, in the promise of this new land.

Like Moses and his generation, they, and successive generations, had to endure frustration and disappointment, difficulty and occasional failure. But they recognized when they assembled for worship and for study that the tradition did not begin on Randolph Street or Willis and Brush, nor even in a meeting between a poor and impoverished group of refugees and a stubborn governor of a Dutch colony by the name of

Peter Stuyvesant. No. When they entered the synagogue, they could hear Abraham and Isaiah and Hillel and Akiva.

The story of Shaarey Zedek congregation can be told in six synagogue buildings, each representing a different chapter of this development. But the current synagogue building is significantly designed in the shape of a mountain. God revealed Himself to man in biblical days on mountaintops, on Mount Moriah and on Mount Sinai, and at the end of life to Moses, on Mount Pisgah. The congregation assembles in the sanctuary on a great mountain peak of the spirit from which we can obtain a better view of our lives. From the heights afforded by the collected wisdom and experience of Israel's poets and prophets, psalmists and sages, preserved in our Torah, instilled through our prayer book, we obtain a higher conception of life, of our responsibilities, of our relationships to one another.

Here we experience the total reality of the Jewish people, a reality not of today or yesterday alone but of all the generations. Where else but in the synagogue and its prayer book, and its Torah of archaic parchment, can I catch echoes of the voices of the generations from whom I am sprung? Here we know that the hand that was placed on our fathers and mothers will not let us go, that we belong to the ages and the ages belong to us. It is here that we perceive the message clearly and directly: "You are not a Jew merely because you were born a Jew or because the non-Jew excludes you from his company. What unites us is not the misunderstanding and hatred of which the Jew has been such a persistent object and victim. We are not primarily a fraternity of the aggrieved, a society of the persecuted, or an agency of relief. We're a community sharing a history, a heritage, a faith, a hope." The synagogue declares that we are a people dedicated to bearing witness to the presence of God, to achieving His purpose by fulfilling His commandments. The synagogue has been the institution which conveys the meaning of Jewish existence.

It is a common mistake to believe that the synagogue is a gathering place for saints. It is not. If it were, it would not be so crowded. By coming to the synagogue, we don't pretend that we are perfect. We recognize that we could be better. We believe that God would not give us a glimpse of something better within our reach without giving us, at the same time, the ability to reach it. At a time when there is so much cynicism, so much corruption, so much violence, we need the synagogue to strengthen our commitment to goodness and compassion and love.

The synagogue therefore has embodied the hope of the Jewish people. It has expressed our hope for the future—not only the faith that there will be a future but also the conviction that the future will be congenial to the ideals and values we cherish.

The founders of Shaarey Zedek and the successive generations that continue their work taught us a profound and enduring truth. None of the agencies or organizations of Jewish life—hospitals, centers, defense organizations, or even federations—are able to perform the most indispensable task upon which everything depends, which is to make Jews Jewish. Only the synagogue has that capacity. The synagogue alone has, as its aim, the program of inculcating from childhood the depth of Jewish identity, the sense of Jewish belonging, and commitment to the Jewish future. The American Jewish community is the source of both material resources and moral strength for the Jews of Israel and the Jews of the Soviet Union. It is the synagogue that has preserved, taught, and renewed a common history. We are linked by a common destiny; we are inspired by a common vision.

Moses could not complete his task. No generation can finish the work. But each generation has reason to be concerned about the future. We face problems and challenges that seem unprecedented. The process of assimilation into American culture has weakened the Jewish ideals and standards to which former generations were loyal. We have paid a very high price for our integration in a free society. The decline in the strength of the Jewish family has serious consequences for a way of life preserved by the transmission of values from parents to children.

On these days, we pray, "Zochraynu l'chayim"—"Remember us to life." We want to live as individuals. We want to live as people. Recently a colleague asked the question, "How is it permitted for us to pray 'Zochraynu l'chayim,' 'Remember us to life,' when we know that in the nature of things, a time must come when that prayer cannot possibly be answered? God cannot always give us another year of life. Many offered that prayer last year who are no longer with us this year." And as I thought about his question, it occurred to me that when we ask "Zochraynu l'chayim," we are asking for more than personal continuity. We are asking for the continuity of the Jewish people, of the congregation with which we pray. We want to live on as the Jewish community.

If we pray for Jewish survival—"Zochraynu l'chayim"—we have to live in such a way that we help to make that prayer come true.

Like Moses, we need to prepare for the next generation to take on the mantle of leadership, for in their loyalty will our hope be fulfilled. A synagogue centers attention upon the education of the young so that children in their earliest formative years may discover the joy and celebration that are linked with their Jewishness. It accompanies its youth through adolescence and young adulthood so that the emotions of childhood may become buttressed by the reason and understanding which come with developing maturity.

We face serious challenges in the days ahead, but we are equal to the tasks that lie before us. As a people, we have withstood persecution and rejection. Can we remain Jews in this land with its climate of tolerance and acceptance? Can the synagogue strengthen our will to accept with faith and courage the responsibilities and burdens that are uniquely ours as Jews, prepared to preserve the best of our heritage and to advance the noblest ideals of America's free society?

The significance of 120 is that these were the years granted to Moses. When he died, the Bible said that his spirit was not diminished, nor was his force abated. He remained vital, strong, and determined every day of his life. Hence, the felicitation in our tradition upon the attainment of a birthday or an anniversary.

Ad maya v'esrim—until 120, the years granted to Moses.

These years were not long enough for Moses to complete his work, but he ascended the mountaintop, and through the mists of the future, he perceived the landscape of hope.

The ethics of the fathers tell us it is not up to us to complete the tasks, but neither are we free to desist from it. Unto Congregation Shaarey Zedek have been granted 120 years of history and of heritage. Let us hold fast to the faith that what we have known and loved will not be lost, that the heritage granted to us will be renewed in the generation of the future. Let us, in sharing this dream, rededicate ourselves to the ideals of the synagogue and ever be worthy of God's blessing and His presence.